CW01652281

GREAT

PASTA SAUCES

GREAT PASTA SAUCES

THE HEART OF ITALIAN COOKING

Linda Fraser

Sebastian Kelly

First published in 1998 by
Sebastian Kelly
2 Rectory Road
Oxford OX4 1BW

Produced by Anness Publishing Limited
Hermes House, 88–89 Blackfriars Road
London SE1 8HA

This edition published in 1998 for Lifetime Distributors Pty Ltd
Building G, 2 Hudson Avenue, Castle Hill NSW 2154
Ph: (02) 9634 1333 Fax: (02) 9634 5955

ISBN 1-84081-013-0

A CIP catalogue record for this book is available from the British Library

Publisher: Joanna Lorenz
Cookery Editors: Rosemary Wilkinson, Linda Doeser
Designers: Bill Mason, Siân Keogh
Illustrator: Anna Koska

Front Cover: Lisa Tai, Designer; Thomas Odulate, Photographer;
Helen Trent, Stylist; Lucy McKelvie, Home Economist

Recipes: Catherine Atkinson, Carla Capalbo, Maxine Clark, Roz Denny, Christine France, Sarah Gates, Shirley Gill, Norma MacMillan, Sue Maggs, Elizabeth Martin, Annie Nichols, Jenny Stacy, Liz Trigg, Laura Washburn, Steven Wheeler
Photographs: Karl Adamson, Edward Allwright, David Armstrong, Steve Baxter, Jo Brewer, James Duncan, Michelle Garrett, Amanda Heywood, Patrick McLeavey, Michael Michaels
Stylists: Madeleine Brehaut, Jo Brewer, Carla Capalbo, Michelle Garrett, Hilary Guy, Amanda Heywood, Patrick McLeavey, Blake Minton, Kirsty Rawlings, Elizabeth Wolf-Cohen
Food for Photography: Wendy Lee, Lucy McKelvie, Jane Stevenson, Elizabeth Wolf-Cohen

Previously published as part of a larger compendium: *Best-Ever Pasta*

Printed in Hong Kong/China

1 3 5 7 9 10 8 6 4 2

NOTES

For all recipes, quantities are given in both metric and imperial measures and, where appropriate, measures are given in standard cups and spoons. Follow one set, but not a mixture, because they are not interchangeable.

Standard spoon and cup measurements are level.
1 tsp = 5ml, 1 tbsp = 15ml; 1 cup = 250ml/8fl oz

Australian standard tablespoons are 20ml. Australian readers should use 3 tsp in place of 1 tbsp for measuring small quantities of gelatine, cornflour, salt etc.

Medium eggs should be used unless otherwise stated.

Contents

Introduction

Virtually anything and everything goes with pasta: meat, poultry, vegetables, fish, seafood, cheese, eggs, cream, herbs. It is one of the world's most versatile and adaptable foods – as well as being nourishing, economic and easy to cook. Sauces for pasta can be as quick and simple or as elaborate and rich as you like.

There are no hard-and-fast rules about what pasta shape to serve with which sauce. However, as a general rule, long, thin, smooth pastas, such as spaghetti, tagliarini and fettuccine, are best suited to lighter and simpler sauces. Short, curly and fluted shapes, such as fusilli (spirals), rigatoni (hollow ridged tubes), farfalle (bows) and penne (quills), will more easily hold thicker, meaty and substantial sauces. Pasta sheets and tubes, such as lasagne and cannelloni, are also suited to rich, thick sauces with which they are baked in the oven. The recipes in this book suggest particular pasta shapes, but you can substitute your own favourites.

The book is divided into four sections, according to the main ingredients of the sauce – Meat & Poultry, Cheese & Cream, Fish & Shellfish, and Vegetables. Some are familiar classics, such as Pasta with Bolognese Sauce, Spaghetti alla Carbonara, Tagliatelle with Gorgonzola Sauce and Pasta Napoletana. Others offer a more unusual and adventurous combination of flavours and textures. Try Linguine with Clams, Leeks and Tomatoes, Fusilli with Turkey, Pasta with Courgette and Walnut Sauce or Greek Pasta with Avocado Sauce; they will soon become firm family favourites, too. Most of the sauces are quick and easy to make – some taking only a few minutes. A few are a little more complicated and time-consuming, but would be a perfect choice for when friends visit.

Types of Pasta

There are thought to be at least 200 different pasta shapes – with about three times as many different names. New shapes and "designer" pasta are being produced all the time. Moreover, the same shape may have a different name in different regions of Italy.

Fresh and dried pasta

Perhaps more importantly, pasta can be categorized as dried and fresh. Many different shapes of dried pasta are readily available from supermarkets. It is probably not worth buying fresh unfilled pasta unless you have access to a really excellent Italian delicatessen. Buying fresh filled pasta, however, is worthwhile.

Basic plain pasta, whether fresh or dried, is made from durum flour, olive oil and eggs. Additional ingredients may colour it. Green, flavoured with spinach,

is the commonest variation. Red pasta is flavoured with tomatoes and black pasta with cuttlefish ink.

Wholemeal pasta may be substituted for ordinary pasta. Made with both wholemeal and plain white flour, it has a firmer texture and contains more fibre.

Cooking Pasta

The secret to cooking perfect pasta is not to overcook it. In Italy it is cooked until it is al dente ("to the tooth"), that is just tender, but still firm to the bite. Make sure that you use a big enough saucepan to hold plenty of boiling water. Allow 3 litres/5¼ pints/12½ cups for each 450 g/1 lb of pasta.

1 Bring a large saucepan of lightly salted water to the boil.

2 Add 15 ml/1 tbsp olive oil. This will prevent the water from boiling over and also stop the pasta from sticking together.

3 Add the pasta to the pan and stir with a wooden spoon to separate. Bring the water back to a rolling boil and cook until the pasta is just tender, but still firm to the bite.

4 Drain in a colander and toss thoroughly in olive oil, butter or your chosen sauce, using two forks to ensure that it is well coated. Alternatively, transfer to a dish and pour the sauce on top.

Cooking Times

Time from the moment the water returns to a rolling boil after you have added the pasta.

Fresh unfilled pasta:	2–3 minutes
Dried unfilled pasta:	8–12 minutes
Fresh filled pasta:	8–10 minutes
Dried filled pasta:	15–20 minutes

These are only guidelines and you should check while the pasta is boiling to avoid overcooking.

Herbs

These are one of the important ingredients in any sauce. It is always better to use fresh rather than dried herbs if possible. However, some dried herbs may be used successfully. As their flavour is concentrated, use only half the quantity specified in the recipe for fresh herbs. Some herbs, particularly the delicate ones, are better frozen than dried.

Choosing herbs
When buying fresh herbs, look for clean, unblemished leaves with a pleasant aroma and a good colour. Depending on the variety, they may be chopped finely or coarsely, torn into pieces or left whole in sprigs. A fresh sprig also makes an attractive garnish. Ideally, fresh herbs should be used immediately after cutting, but this is not always possible. Most can be stored for a short while in the refrigerator with their stems in a jar of water and covered with a plastic bag.

Basil
This is the classic herb for pasta sauces. It has a warm, pungent aroma and flavour, and the leaves are soft and shiny. They are best torn by hand, rather than chopped, as this retains more flavour. The most frequently available type of basil is also known as sweet basil. Other varieties include Neapolitana, which has large, crinkled leaves and a very strong flavour that makes it perfect for pesto. There are also several purple varieties. Basil is the ideal herb for tomato sauces, delicate ricotta cheese fillings, and fish and poultry sauces. It is, of course, a main ingredient in pesto and can simply be used with garlic and olive oil to dress freshly cooked pasta for a quick and easy lunch. It is not suitable for hearty meat sauces, which will drown its flavour. Dried basil is a poor substitute for fresh, lacking in both pungency and colour. If you cannot obtain fresh basil, use a spoonful of ready-made pesto sauce instead.

Bay leaves
The bay is a member of the laurel family and, as it is evergreen, fresh leaves are available all year. They are firm and shiny with a dull underside. Dried bay leaves are a satisfactory substitute. Strongly fragrant, bay leaves are used to flavour meat sauces and béchamel or white sauces in baked dishes.

Coriander
Similar to flat leaf parsley in appearance, coriander has an intense fragrance and delicious flavour. It is usually used roughly chopped and fresh sprigs make a very attractive garnish. It goes well with most ingredients, including poultry and meat.

Dill
The feathery leaves have a distinctive, aniseed-like flavour. Traditionally used to flavour fish sauces, it also goes well with cream cheese and cucumber.

Marjoram and organo
These herbs belong to the same family; oregano is also known as wild marjoram. It has a stronger flavour than sweet marjoram. They are among the most popular herbs in the Italian kitchen. They keep their flavour well when dried. Both go well with tomato and egg sauces, as well as meat, fish and poultry. When in flower, they make an unusual and appealing garnish.

Mint
There are many different varieties of mint. Some, like apple or pineapple mint, have an overlying flavour. Mint is a popular herb in Italy for using with fish.

Parsley
This a very versatile, almost all-purpose herb. It has a fresh, "green" taste that goes well with meat, poultry, fish and vegetable sauces. A delicious pesto sauce can be made using parsley instead of basil. There are two varieties, curly and flat leaf. There is little difference in the flavour. Curly parsley is usually finely chopped, while the flat leaf variety is better coarsely chopped.

Rosemary
The dark green, needle-like leaves of rosemary are intensely aromatic with a very powerful flavour, so it should be used with discretion. The resinous oils ensure that dried rosemary is almost as pungent as fresh. It is traditionally used to flavour lamb, but also goes well with pork. The needles are extremely tough, so they should be very finely chopped.

Sage
Together with basil, oregano and marjoram, sage is one of the most popular Italian herbs. Fresh sage is strongly flavoured and very aromatic. Dried sage is not a very satisfactory substitute and tends to become dusty. Sage goes well with strongly flavoured ingredients, such as meat, garlic, tomatoes and Gorgonzola cheese. It is frequently used in stuffed pasta dishes from the Emilia-Romagna region. There are many varieties, including ones with variegated leaves.

Thyme
The tiny, grey-green leaves are extremely pungent and very aromatic, as they contain highly concentrated, volatile essential oils. There are many varieties of thyme, ranging from wild thyme to spicy lemon and orange. Common thyme goes well with meat sauces, and lemon thyme is delicious with fish and seafood.

Chopping herbs
For finely chopped herbs, pull the leaves off the stems and pile them together on a chopping board. With one hand, hold down the point of a sharp knife to act as a pivot, and chop backwards and forwards across the leaves. Alternatively, you can use a special herb chopper called a mezzaluna. This double-handled blade is simply rocked over the pile of leaves from side to side.

For coarsely chopped herbs, hold the leaves in one hand bunched against the blade of a sharp knife. Chop with the knife against your fingers – with care.

Some herbs are most easily prepared by snipping them with kitchen scissors. Basil leaves are usually coarsely torn by hand.

Basic Sauce Ingredients

There is no need to buy expensive and sophisticated ingredients to make delicious pasta sauces. However, it is worth taking note of some typically Italian or other especially useful ingredients.

Clams
There are many different varieties of clams found in the coastal waters of almost every continent. The tiny variety, known in Italy as *vongole*, are best for pasta sauces. If fresh clams are unavailable, you could substitute fresh cockles or clams canned in brine.

Dolcelatte
This blue-veined, semi-soft Italian cheese has a delicate, piquant flavour and a creamy texture. It is used in sauces and pasta fillings.

Feta
This Greek cheese is traditionally made from ewe's milk, but now is more frequently made from cow's milk. It is crumbly with a bland, slightly salty flavour, as it is preserved in brine. It is usually sold vacuum packed and is produced by many other countries as well.

Gorgonzola
One of the oldest blue-veined cheeses in the world, Gorgonzola is semi-soft, creamy and piquant in flavour. It should have a distinctive but not bitter smell.

Italian sausages
These are highly seasoned and meaty, ranging in size from about 50 g/2 oz to 1 kg/2¼ lb. Varieties include *cervellata*, a pork sausage flavoured with Parmesan cheese and saffron, and *cotechino*, pork flavoured with white wine, cloves and cinnamon. Squeeze the meat from the casing to make easy sauces and stuffings.

Mediterranean prawns
About 20–23 cm/8–9 inches long, these have more flavour than smaller varieties. They are available raw and cooked. Make sure frozen prawns are fully thawed.

Mussels
Fresh mussels are best, and they should be cooked on the day of purchase. Frozen cooked mussels may be used as a substitute.

Nuts
Pistachios and walnuts are excellent for colouring and flavouring a variety of sauces.

Olives
Olives are used to add richness to sauces. Black olives have a stronger flavour than green.

Onions
Used to add a strong undertone to sauces made with meat, fish and vegetables, onions are essential in the Italian kitchen. Red onions have a mild flavour and look attractive. Spanish onions are sweeter than other varieties.

Pancetta
This Italian bacon adds flavour to sauces and is a traditional ingredient in such classic recipes as spaghetti alla carbonara. It may be smoked or unsmoked, sliced or in a single piece. If you cannot obtain it, substitute streaky bacon, but the flavour will be less powerful.

Parmesan cheese
This hard cheese comes from a specified area in north-central Italy and the rind is always stamped

with *Parmigiano Reggiano* as a guarantee of its origin. It has a grainy texture and a fragrant flavour. Grated Parmesan or thin shavings are sprinkled over many pasta sauces just before serving or at the table. It is better to buy Parmesan cheese in a single piece and grate it freshly as required.

Peppers
Available in a variety of colours, peppers are a tasty and colourful

addition to pasta sauces. Red, yellow and orange peppers are sweeter than green ones.

Pine nuts
Small, cream-coloured and very oily, pine nuts are essential for making pesto sauce. They do not keep well.

Ricotta
This Italian whey cheese is creamy and white with a smooth, soft texture and a bland, slightly sweet flavour. It is very versatile and used with ingredients, such as spinach and nuts, for pasta stuffings.

Smoked salmon
Thinly sliced smoked salmon is a quick and easy addition both to sauces and pasta stuffings.

Spinach
The deep green, iron-rich leaves are used to colour pasta, as well as for making sauces and stuffings. Young spinach leaves are the most tender.

Tomatoes
Buy fresh tomatoes that are really ripe. Typically Italian, plum tomatoes have a concentrated flavour and less watery flesh than many other varieties, making them ideal for pasta sauces. Miniature or cherry tomatoes are also excellent in pasta sauces. Canned plum tomatoes are a useful stand-by.

Meat & Poultry Sauces

Pasta with Bolognese Sauce

Traditional Bolognese sauce contains chicken livers to add richness, but you can leave them out and replace with an equal quantity of minced beef.

INGREDIENTS

Serves 4–6

75g/3oz pancetta or bacon
115g/4oz chicken livers
50g/2oz/4 tbsp butter, plus extra for tossing the pasta
1 onion, finely chopped
1 carrot, diced
1 celery stick, finely chopped
225g/8oz/2 cups lean minced beef
30ml/2 tbsp tomato purée
120ml/4fl oz/½ cup white wine
200ml/7fl oz/scant 1 cup beef stock or water
freshly grated nutmeg
450g/1lb tagliatelle, spaghetti or fettuccine
salt and ground black pepper
freshly grated Parmesan cheese, to serve

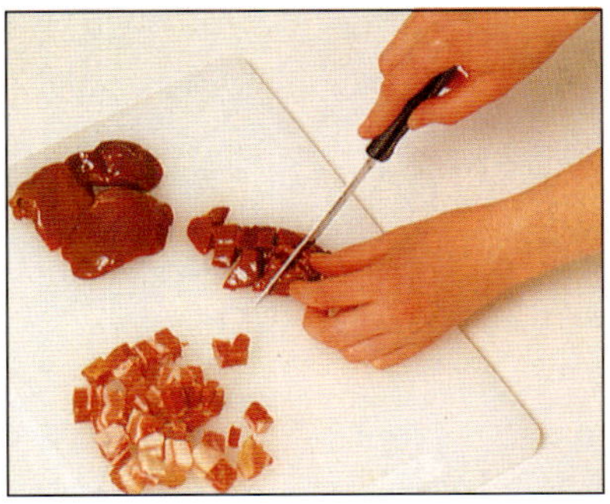

1 Dice the pancetta or bacon. Trim the chicken livers, removing any fat or gristle and any "green" bits which will be bitter if left on. Roughly chop the livers.

2 Melt 50g/2oz/4 tbsp butter in a saucepan and add the bacon. Cook for 2-3 minutes until just beginning to brown. Then add the onion, carrot and celery and brown these too.

3 Stir in the beef and brown over a high heat, breaking it up with a spoon. Add the chicken livers and cook for 2-3 minutes. Add the tomato purée with the wine and stock or water. Season well with salt, pepper and nutmeg. Bring to the boil, cover and simmer for 35 minutes.

4 Cook the pasta in plenty of boiling salted water according to the instructions on the packet or until *al dente*. Drain well and toss with the extra butter. Toss the meat sauce with the pasta and serve with plenty of grated Parmesan cheese.

Pasta Spirals with Chicken and Tomato

A recipe for a speedy supper – serve this dish with a mixed bean salad.

INGREDIENTS

Serves 4

15ml/1 tbsp olive oil
1 onion, chopped
1 carrot, chopped
50g/2oz sun-dried tomatoes in olive oil, drained weight
1 garlic clove, chopped
400g/14oz can chopped tomatoes, drained
15ml/1 tbsp tomato purée
150ml/¼ pint/⅔ cup chicken stock
350g/12oz fusilli
225g/8oz chicken, diagonally sliced
salt and ground black pepper
fresh mint sprigs, to garnish

1 Heat the oil in a large frying pan and fry the onion and carrot for 5 minutes, stirring the vegetables occasionally.

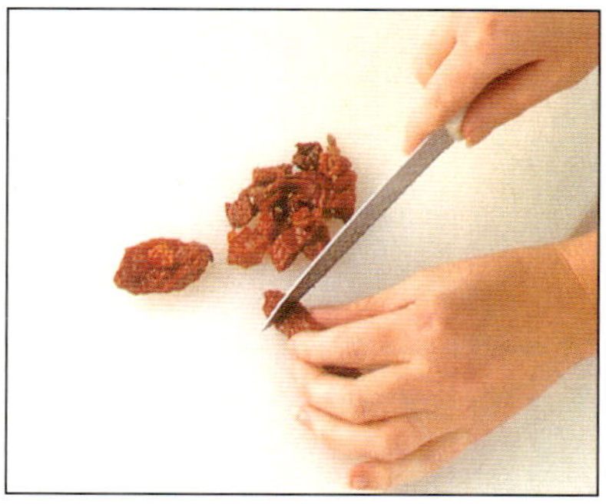

2 Chop the sun-dried tomatoes and set aside until needed.

3 Stir the garlic, tomatoes, tomato purée and stock into the onions and carrots and bring to the boil. Simmer for 10 minutes, stirring occasionally.

4 Cook the pasta in plenty of boiling salted water according to the instructions on the packet.

5 Pour the sauce into a blender or food processor and process until smooth.

6 Return the sauce to the pan and stir in the sun-dried tomatoes and chicken. Bring back to the boil and then simmer for 10 minutes until the chicken is cooked. Adjust the seasoning, if necessary.

7 Drain the pasta thoroughly and toss in the sauce. Serve at once, garnished with sprigs of fresh mint.

Spirali with Smoky Bacon Sauce

A wonderful sauce to prepare in mid-summer when the tomatoes are ripe and sweet.

INGREDIENTS

Serves 4

900g/2lb ripe tomatoes
6 rashers smoked streaky bacon
50g/2oz/4 tbsp butter
1 onion, chopped
15ml/1 tbsp chopped fresh oregano or 5ml/1 tsp dried
450g/1lb pasta, any variety
salt and ground black pepper
freshly grated Parmesan cheese, to serve

1 Plunge the tomatoes into boiling water for 1 minute, then into cold water. Slip off the skins. Halve the tomatoes, remove the seeds and cores and roughly chop the flesh.

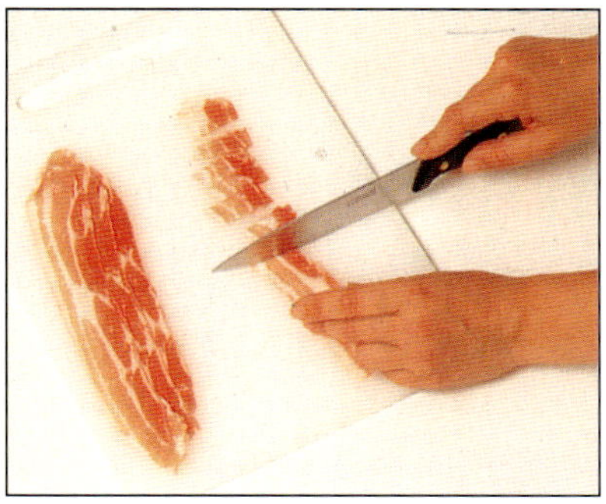

2 Remove the rind from the streaky bacon and roughly chop the meat.

3 Melt the butter in a saucepan and add the bacon. Fry until lightly browned, then add the onion and cook gently for 5 minutes until softened. Add the tomatoes, salt, pepper and oregano. Simmer gently for 10 minutes.

4 Cook the pasta in plenty of boiling salted water according to the instructions on the packet. Drain well and toss with the sauce. Serve with plenty of freshly grated Parmesan cheese.

Spaghetti with Bacon and Tomato Sauce

This substantial sauce is a meal in itself, so serve it up as a warming winter supper.

INGREDIENTS

Serves 4

15ml/1 tbsp olive oil
225g/8oz smoked streaky bacon, rinded and roughly chopped
250g/9oz spaghetti
5ml/1 tsp chilli powder
1 quantity Classic Tomato Sauce (see Curly Lasagne with Classic Tomato Sauce)
salt and ground black pepper
roughly chopped fresh flat leaf parsley, to garnish

1 Heat the oil in large frying pan and fry the bacon for about 10 minutes, stirring occasionally until crisp and golden.

2 Cook the pasta following the instructions on the packet, until *al dente*.

3 Add the chilli powder to the bacon and cook for 2 minutes. Stir in the tomato sauce and bring to the boil. Cover and simmer for 10 minutes. Season with salt and pepper to taste.

4 Drain the pasta thoroughly and toss it together with the sauce. Serve garnished with the roughly chopped fresh parsley.

Tagliatelle with Pea and Ham Sauce

A colourful sauce, this is ideal served with crusty Italian or French bread.

INGREDIENTS

Serves 4

350g/12oz tagliatelle
225g/8oz/1½ cups shelled peas
300ml/½ pint/1¼ cups single cream
50g/2oz/⅓ cup freshly grated fontina cheese
75g/3oz Parma ham, sliced into strips
salt and ground black pepper

1 Cook the pasta following the instructions on the packet until *al dente*.

2 Plunge the peas into a pan of boiling salted water and cook for about 7 minutes or until tender. Drain and set aside.

3 Place the cream and half the fontina cheese in a small saucepan and heat gently, stirring constantly until heated through.

4 Drain the pasta thoroughly and turn it into a large serving bowl. Toss together the pasta, ham and peas and pour on the sauce. Add the remaining cheese and season with salt and pepper to taste.

Rigatoni with Spicy Sausage

This is really a cheat's Bolognese sauce using the wonderful fresh spicy sausages sold in every good Italian delicatessen.

INGREDIENTS

Serves 4

450g/1lb fresh spicy Italian sausage
30ml/2 tbsp olive oil
1 onion, chopped
450ml/¾ pint/1¾ cups passata
150ml/¼ pint/⅔ cup dry red wine
6 sun-dried tomatoes in oil, drained
450g/1lb rigatoni or similar pasta
salt and ground black pepper
freshly grated Parmesan cheese, to serve

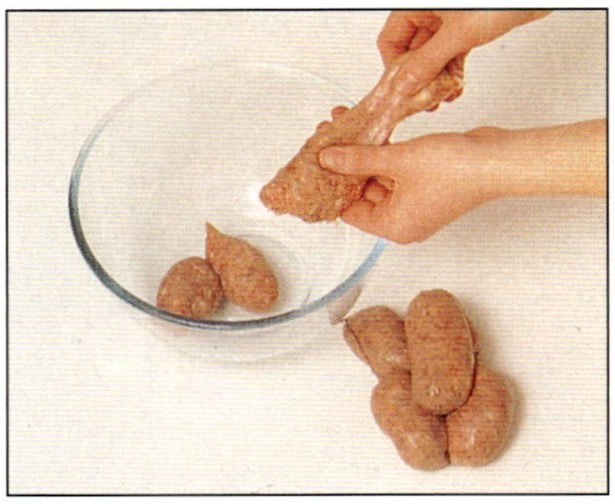

1 Squeeze the sausages out of their skins into a bowl and break up the meat.

2 Heat the oil in a medium saucepan and add the onion. Cook for 5 minutes until soft and golden. Stir in the sausagemeat, browning it all over and breaking up the lumps with a wooden spoon. Pour in the passata and the wine. Bring to the boil.

3 Slice the sun-dried tomatoes and add to the sauce. Simmer for 3 minutes until reduced, stirring occasionally. Season.

4 Cook the pasta in plenty of boiling salted water according to the instructions on the packet. Drain well and top with the sauce. Serve with Parmesan cheese.

Spicy Beef

If you are hungry and only have a few minutes to spare for cooking, this colourful and healthy dish is an excellent choice.

INGREDIENTS

Serves 4

15ml/1 tbsp oil
450g/1lb/4 cups minced beef
2.5cm/1in piece fresh root ginger, sliced
5ml/1 tsp Chinese five-spice powder
1 red chilli, sliced
50g/2oz mange-touts
1 red pepper, seeded and chopped
1 carrot, sliced
115g/4oz beansprouts
15ml/1 tbsp sesame oil
cooked Chinese egg noodles, to serve

1 Heat the oil in a wok until almost smoking. Add the minced beef and cook for about 3 minutes, stirring all the time.

2 Add the ginger, Chinese five-spice powder and chilli. Cook for 1 minute.

3 Add the mange-touts, the seeded and chopped red pepper and sliced carrot and cook for a further 3 minutes, stirring the mixture continuously.

4 Add the beansprouts and sesame oil and cook for a final 2 minutes. Serve immediately with Chinese egg noodles.

Tagliatelle with Parma Ham and Asparagus

A stunning sauce, this is worth every effort to serve at a dinner party.

INGREDIENTS

Serves 4

- 350g/12oz tagliatelle
- 25g/1oz/2 tbsp butter
- 15ml/1 tbsp olive oil
- 225g/8oz asparagus tips
- 1 garlic clove, chopped
- 115g/4oz Parma ham, sliced into strips
- 30ml/2 tbsp chopped fresh sage
- 150ml/¼ pint/⅔ cup single cream
- 115g/4oz/1 cup grated chive-and-onion double Gloucester cheese
- 115g/4oz/1 cup grated Gruyère cheese
- salt and ground black pepper
- fresh sage sprigs, to garnish

1 Cook the pasta in plenty of boiling salted water according to the instructions on the packet.

2 Melt the butter and oil in a frying pan and gently fry the asparagus tips for about 5 minutes, stirring occasionally, until they are almost tender.

3 Stir in the garlic and Parma ham and fry for 1 minute.

4 Stir in the chopped sage and fry for a further 1 minute.

5 Pour in the cream and bring the mixture to the boil.

6 Add the cheeses and simmer gently, stirring occasionally, until thoroughly melted. Season.

7 Drain the pasta thoroughly and toss with the sauce to coat. Serve immediately, garnished with fresh sage sprigs.

Peasant Bolognese

A spicy version of a popular dish. Worcestershire sauce and chorizo sausages add an extra element to this perfect family standby.

INGREDIENTS

Serves 4

15ml/1 tbsp oil
225g/8oz/2 cups minced beef
1 onion, chopped
5ml/1 tsp chilli powder
15ml/1 tbsp Worcestershire sauce
25g/1oz/2 tbsp plain flour
150ml/¼ pint/⅔ cup beef stock
4 chorizo sausages
50g/2oz baby sweetcorn
200g/7oz can chopped tomatoes
15ml/1 tbsp chopped fresh basil
salt and ground black pepper
cooked spaghetti, to serve
fresh basil, to garnish

1 Heat the oil in a large pan and fry the minced beef for 5 minutes. Add the onion and chilli powder and cook for a further 3 minutes.

2 Stir in the Worcestershire sauce and flour. Cook for 1 minute before pouring in the stock.

3 Slice the chirozo sausages and halve the corn lengthways.

4 Stir in the sausages, tomatoes, sweetcorn and chopped basil. Season well and bring to the boil. Reduce the heat and simmer for 30 minutes. Serve with spaghetti, garnished with fresh basil.

COOK'S TIP

Make up the Bolognese sauce and freeze in conveniently sized portions for up to two months.

Tagliatelle with Chicken and Herb Sauce

Serve this delicious dish with its wine-flavoured sauce and a fresh green salad.

INGREDIENTS

Serves 4

30ml/2 tbsp olive oil
1 red onion, cut into wedges
350g/12oz tagliatelle
1 garlic clove, chopped
350g/12oz chicken, diced
300ml/½ pint/1¼ cups dry vermouth
45ml/3 tbsp chopped fresh mixed herbs
150ml/¼ pint/⅔ cup fromage frais
salt and ground black pepper
shredded fresh mint, to garnish

1 Heat the oil in a large frying pan and fry the red onion for 10 minutes until softened and the layers have separated.

2 Cook the pasta in plenty of boiling salted water according to the instructions on the packet.

3 Add the garlic and chicken to the frying pan and fry for 10 minutes, stirring occasionally, until the chicken is browned all over and cooked through.

4 Pour in the vermouth, bring to boiling point and boil rapidly until reduced by about half.

5 Stir in the herbs, fromage frais and seasoning and heat through gently, but do not boil.

6 Drain the pasta thoroughly and toss with the sauce to coat. Serve immediately, garnished with shredded fresh mint.

Spaghetti in a Cream and Bacon Sauce

This is a light and creamy sauce flavoured with bacon and lightly cooked eggs.

INGREDIENTS

Serves 4

350g/12oz spaghetti
15ml/1 tbsp olive oil
1 onion, chopped
115g/4oz rindless streaky bacon or pancetta, diced
1 garlic clove, chopped
3 eggs
300ml/½ pint/1¼ cups double cream
50g/2oz Parmesan cheese
chopped fresh basil, to garnish

1 Cook the pasta in plenty of boiling salted water according to the instructions on the packet.

2 Heat the oil in a frying pan and fry the onion and bacon or pancetta for 10 minutes, until softened. Stir in the garlic and fry for a further 2 minutes, stirring occasionally.

3 Meanwhile, beat the eggs in a bowl, then stir in the cream and seasoning. Grate the Parmesan cheese and stir into the egg and cream mixture.

4 Stir the cream mixture into the onion and bacon or pancetta and cook over a low heat for a few minutes, stirring constantly, until heated through. Season to taste.

5 Drain the pasta thoroughly and turn into a large serving dish. Pour over the sauce and toss to coat. Serve immediately, garnished with chopped fresh basil.

Rigatoni with Garlic Crumbs

A hot and spicy dish – halve the quantity of chilli if you like a milder flavour. The bacon is an optional addition; you can leave it out if you are cooking for vegetarians.

INGREDIENTS

Serves 4–6

45ml/3 tbsp olive oil
2 shallots, chopped
8 rashers streaky bacon, chopped (optional)
10ml/2 tsp crushed dried red chillies
400g/14oz can chopped tomatoes with garlic and herbs
6 slices white bread
115g/4oz/½ cup butter
2 garlic cloves, chopped
450g/1lb rigatoni
salt and ground black pepper

1 Heat the oil in a medium saucepan and fry the shallots and bacon, if using, gently for 6–8 minutes until golden. Add the dried chillies and chopped tomatoes, half-cover and simmer for 20 minutes.

2 Meanwhile, cut the crusts off the bread and discard them. Reduce the bread to crumbs in a blender or food processor.

3 Heat the butter in a frying pan, add the garlic and bread-crumbs and stir-fry until golden and crisp. (Don't let the crumbs catch and burn or the final result will be ruined.)

4 Cook the pasta in plenty of boiling salted water according to the instructions on the packet, until *al dente*. Drain well.

5 Toss the pasta with the tomato sauce and divide among four or six warmed serving plates.

6 Sprinkle with the crumbs and serve immediately.

Pasta Twists with Classic Meat Sauce

This is a rich meat sauce which is ideal to serve with all types of pasta. The sauce definitely improves if kept overnight in the fridge. This allows the flavours time to mature.

INGREDIENTS

Serves 4

450g/1lb/4 cups minced beef
115g/4oz smoked streaky beacon, rinded and chopped
1 onion, chopped
2 celery sticks, chopped
15ml/1 tbsp plain flour
150ml/¼ pint/⅔ cup chicken stock or water
45ml/3 tbsp tomato purée
1 garlic clove, chopped
45ml/3 tbsp chopped fresh mixed herbs, such as oregano, parsley, marjoram and chives or 15ml/1 tbsp dried mixed herbs
15ml/1 tbsp redcurrant jelly
350g/12oz pasta twists, such as spirali
salt and ground black pepper
chopped oregano, to garnish

1 Heat a large saucepan and fry the beef and bacon for about 10 minutes, stirring occasionally until browned.

2 Add the chopped onion and celery and cook for 2 minutes, stirring occasionally.

3 Stir in the flour and cook for 2 minutes, stirring constantly.

4 Pour in the stock or water and bring to the boil.

5 Stir in the tomato purée, garlic, herbs, redcurrant jelly and seasoning. Bring to the boil, cover and simmer for about 30 minutes.

6 Cook the pasta in plenty of boiling salted water according to the instructions on the packet. Drain thoroughly and turn into a large serving dish. Pour over the sauce and toss to coat. Serve the pasta immediately, garnished with chopped fresh oregano.

COOK'S TIP

The redcurrant jelly helps to draw out the flavour of the tomato purée. You can use a sweet mint jelly or chutney instead, if you like

Pasta Tubes with Meat and Cheese Sauce

The two sauces complement each other perfectly in this wonderfully flavoursome dish.

INGREDIENTS

Serves 4

350g/12oz rigatoni
salt and ground black pepper
fresh basil sprigs, to garnish

For the meat sauce

15ml/1 tbsp olive oil
350g/12oz/3 cups minced beef
1 onion, chopped
1 garlic clove, chopped
400g/14oz can chopped tomatoes
15ml/1 tbsp dried mixed herbs
30ml/2 tbsp tomato purée

For the cheese sauce

50g/2oz/¼ cup butter
50g/2oz/½ cup plain flour
450ml/¾ pint/1¾ cups milk
2 egg yolks
50g/2oz/½ cup freshly grated Parmesan cheese

1 To make the meat sauce, heat the oil in a large frying pan and fry the beef for 10 minutes, stirring occasionally until browned. Add the onion and cook for 5 minutes, stirring occasionally.

2 Stir in the garlic, tomatoes, herbs and tomato purée. Bring to the boil, cover, and simmer for about 30 minutes.

3 Meanwhile, to make the cheese sauce, melt the butter in a small saucepan, then stir in the flour and cook for 2 minutes, stirring constantly.

4 Remove the pan from the heat and gradually stir in the milk. Return the pan to the heat and bring to the boil, stirring occasionally, until thickened.

5 Add the egg yolks, cheese and seasoning and stir until the sauce is well blended.

6 Preheat the grill. Meanwhile, cook the pasta in plenty of boiling salted water according to the instructions on the packet. Drain thoroughly and turn into a large mixing bowl. Pour over the meat sauce and toss to coat.

7 Divide the pasta among four flameproof dishes. Spoon over the cheese sauce and place under the grill until brown. Serve immediately, garnished with fresh basil.

Spaghetti alla Carbonara

It has been said that this dish was originally cooked by Italian coal miners or charcoal-burners, hence the name "carbonara". The secret of its creamy sauce is not to overcook the egg.

INGREDIENTS

Serves 4

175g/6oz unsmoked streaky bacon
1 garlic clove, chopped
3 eggs
450g/1lb spaghetti
60ml/4 tbsp freshly grated Parmesan cheese
salt and ground black pepper

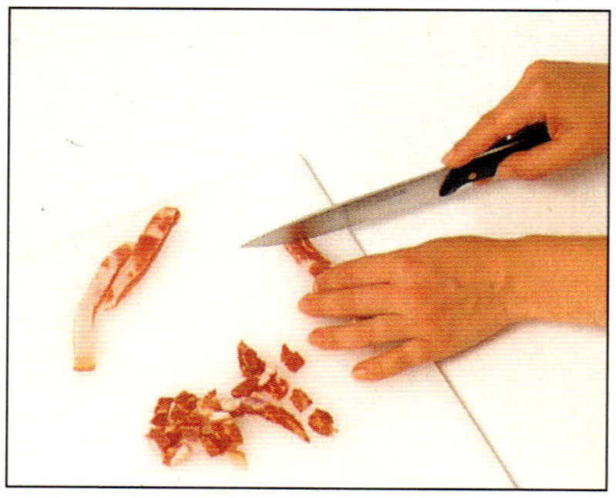

1 Dice the bacon and place in a medium saucepan. Fry in its own fat with the garlic until brown. Keep warm until needed.

2 Whisk the eggs together in a mixing bowl.

3 Cook the spaghetti in plenty of boiling salted water according to the instructions on the packet or until *al dente*. Drain well.

4 Quickly turn the spaghetti into the pan with the bacon and stir in the eggs, a little salt, lots of pepper and half the cheese. Toss well to mix. The eggs should half-cook in the heat from the pasta. Serve in warmed bowls with the remaining Parmesan cheese sprinkled over each portion.

Penne with Sausage and Parmesan Sauce

Spicy sausage tossed in a cheesy tomato sauce is delicious served on a bed of cooked pasta.

INGREDIENTS

Serves 4

350g/12oz penne
450g/1lb ripe tomatoes
30ml/2 tbsp olive oil
225g/8oz chorizo sausage, diagonally sliced
1 garlic clove, chopped
30ml/2 tbsp chopped fresh flat leaf parsley
grated rind of 1 lemon
50g/2oz/½ cup freshly grated Parmesan cheese
salt and ground black pepper
finely chopped fresh flat leaf parsley, to garnish

1 Cook the pasta in plenty of boiling salted water according to the instructions on the packet.

2 Slash the bottoms of the tomatoes with a knife, making a cross. Place in a large bowl, cover with boiling water and leave to stand for 45 seconds. Plunge into cold water for 30 seconds, then peel off the skins and roughly chop the flesh.

3 Heat the oil in a frying pan and fry the sliced chorizo sausage for 5 minutes, stirring from time to time, until browned.

4 Add the chopped tomatoes, garlic, parsley and grated lemon rind. Heat through gently, stirring, for 1 minute.

5 Add the grated Parmesan cheese and season to taste.

6 Drain the pasta well through a colander and toss it with the sauce to coat. Serve immediately, garnished with finely chopped fresh flat leaf parsley.

Noodles with Pancetta and Mushrooms

Porcini mushrooms give this sauce a wonderful depth.

INGREDIENTS

Serves 2–4

25g/1oz dried Italian mushrooms (porcini)
175ml/6fl oz/¾ cup warm water
900g/2lb tomatoes, peeled, seeded and chopped or drained canned tomatoes
1.5ml/¼ tsp dried hot chilli flakes
45ml/3 tbsp olive oil
4 slices pancetta or rashers unsmoked back bacon, cut into thin strips
1 large garlic clove, finely chopped
350g/12oz tagliatelle or fettuccine
salt and ground black pepper
freshly grated Parmesan cheese, to serve

1 Put the mushrooms in a bowl and cover with the warm water. Leave to soak for 20 minutes.

2 Meanwhile, put the tomatoes in a saucepan with the chilli flakes and seasoning. If using canned tomatoes, crush them coarsely with a fork or potato masher. Bring to the boil, reduce the heat and simmer for about 30–40 minutes, until reduced to 750ml/1¼ pints/3 cups. Stir from time to time to prevent sticking.

3 When the mushrooms have finished soaking, lift them out and squeeze the remaining liquid over the bowl; set aside.

4 Carefully pour the soaking liquid into the tomatoes through a muslin-lined sieve. Simmer the tomatoes for a further 15 minutes.

5 Meanwhile, heat 30ml/2 tbsp of the oil in a frying pan. Add the strips of pancetta or bacon and fry until golden but not crisp. Add the garlic and mushrooms and fry for 3 minutes, stirring. Set aside.

6 Cook the pasta in plenty of boiling salted water until just *al dente.*

7 Add the bacon and mushroom mixture to the tomato sauce and mix well. Season with salt and ground black pepper.

8 Drain the pasta and return to the pan. Add the remaining oil and toss to coat the strands. Divide among hot plates, spoon the sauce on top and serve with freshly grated Parmesan cheese.

Pasta Spirals with Pepperoni and Tomato

A warming supper dish, perfect for a cold winter's night. All types of sausage are suitable, but if using raw sausages, add them with the onion to cook thoroughly.

INGREDIENTS

Serves 4

1 onion
1 red pepper
1 green pepper
30ml/2 tbsp olive oil, plus extra for tossing the pasta
800g/1¾ lb canned chopped tomatoes
30ml/2 tbsp tomato purée
10ml/2 tsp paprika
175g/6oz pepperoni or chorizo sausage
45ml/3 tbsp chopped fresh parsley
450g/1lb pasta spirals, such as fusilli
salt and ground black pepper

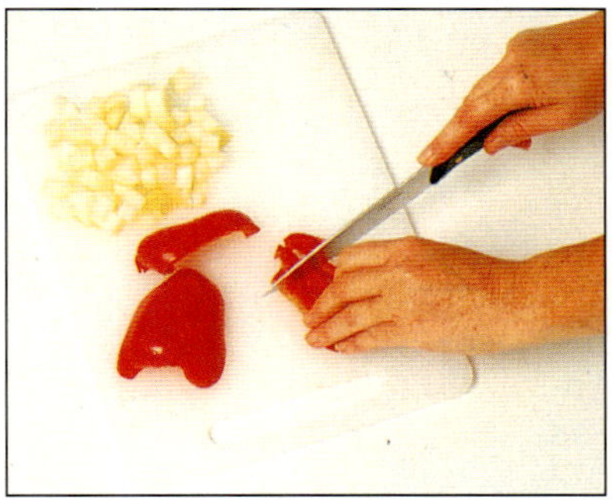

1 Chop the onion. Halve, core and seed the peppers. Cut the flesh into dice.

2 Heat the oil in a medium saucepan, add the onion and cook for 2–3 minutes until beginning to colour. Stir in the peppers, tomatoes, tomato purée and paprika, bring to the boil and simmer uncovered for about 15–20 minutes until reduced and thickened.

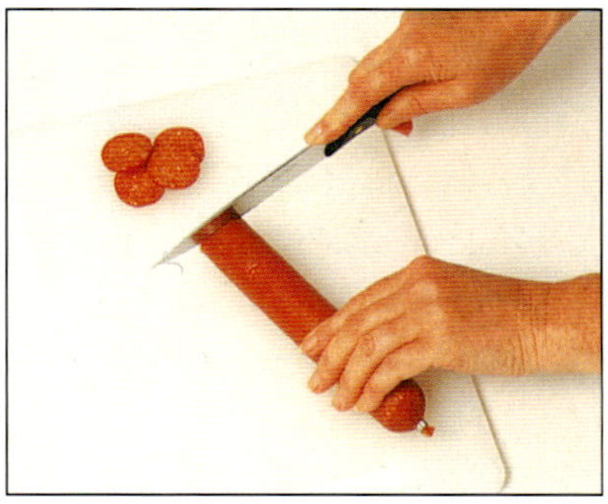

3 Slice the pepperoni or chorizo and stir into the sauce with 30ml/2 tbsp of the chopped parsley. Season to taste with salt and pepper.

4 While the sauce is simmering, cook the pasta in plenty of boiling salted water according to the instructions on the packet. Drain well. Toss the pasta with the remaining parsley in a little extra olive oil. Divide among four warmed bowls and top with sauce.

Pasta with Devilled Kidneys

Ask your butcher to prepare the kidneys for you if you prefer.

INGREDIENTS

Serves 4

8–10 lambs' kidneys
15ml/1 tbsp sunflower oil
25g/1oz/2 tbsp butter
10ml/2 tsp paprika
5–10ml/1–2 tsp mild grainy mustard
salt, to taste
chopped fresh parsley, to garnish
225g/8oz fresh pasta, to serve

1 Cut the kidneys in half and neatly cut out the white cores with scissors. Cut the kidneys again if very large.

2 Heat the oil and butter together. Add the kidneys and cook, turning frequently, for about 2 minutes. Blend the paprika and mustard together with a little salt and stir into the pan.

3 Continue cooking the kidneys, basting frequently, for about a further 3–4 minutes.

4 Cook the pasta for about 10–12 minutes, or according to the instructions on the packet. Serve the kidneys and their sauce, topped with the chopped fresh parsley, and accompanied by the pasta.

Golden-topped Pasta

When it comes to the children helping you to plan the menus, this is the sort of dish that always wins hands down. It is also perfect for "padding out" if you have to feed eight instead of four people.

INGREDIENTS

Serves 4–6

225g/8oz dried pasta shells or spirals
115g/4oz/⅔ cup chopped ham, beef or turkey
350g/12oz par-cooked mixed vegetables, such as carrots, cauliflower, beans, etc
a little oil

For the cheese sauce

25g/1oz/2 tbsp butter
25g/1oz/2 tbsp plain flour
300ml/½ pint/1¼ cups milk
175g/6oz/1½ cups grated Cheddar cheese
5–10ml/1–2 tsp mustard
salt and ground black pepper

1 Cook the pasta according to the instructions on the packet. Drain and place in a flameproof dish with the chopped meat, the vegetables and 5–10ml/1–2 tsp oil.

2 Melt the butter in a saucepan, stir in the flour and cook for 1 minute, stirring. Remove from the heat and gradually stir in the milk. Return to the heat, bring to the boil, stirring and cook for 2 minutes. Add half the cheese, the mustard and seasoning to taste.

3 Spoon the sauce over the meat and vegetables. Sprinkle with the rest of the cheese and grill quickly until golden and bubbling.

Cannelloni with Spinach and Cheese Sauce

This version of a classic Italian dish introduces a variety of vegetables which are topped with a traditional cheese sauce.

INGREDIENTS

Serves 4

8 cannelloni tubes
115g/4oz spinach

For the filling

15ml/1 tbsp oil
175g/6oz/1½ cups minced beef
2 garlic cloves, crushed
25g/1oz/2 tbsp plain flour
120ml/4fl oz/½ cup beef stock
1 small carrot, finely chopped
1 small yellow courgette, chopped
salt and ground black pepper

For the sauce

25g/1oz/2 tbsp butter
25g/1oz/2 tbsp plain flour
250ml/8fl oz/1 cup milk
50g/2oz/½ cup freshly grated Parmesan cheese

1 Preheat the oven to 180°C/350°F/Gas 4. For the filling, heat the oil in a large pan. Add the minced beef and garlic. Cook for 5 minutes.

2 Add the flour and cook for a further 1 minute. Slowly stir in the stock and bring to the boil.

3 Add the carrot and courgette. Season. Cook for 10 minutes.

4 Spoon the mince mixture into the cannelloni tubes and place in an ovenproof dish.

5 Blanch the spinach in boiling water for 3 minutes. Drain well and place on top of the cannelloni tubes in the dish.

6 For the sauce melt the butter in a pan. Add the flour and cook for 1 minute. Pour in the milk, add the grated cheese and season well. Bring to the boil, stirring all the time. Pour over the cannelloni and spinach and bake for 30 minutes. Serve with tomatoes and a crisp green salad, if liked.

Penne with Chicken and Ham Sauce

A meal in itself, this colourful pasta sauce is perfect for lunch or supper.

INGREDIENTS

Serves 4

350g/12oz penne
25g/1oz/2 tbsp butter
1 onion, chopped
1 garlic clove, chopped
1 bay leaf
450ml/¾ pint/1¾ cups dry white wine
150ml/¼ pint/⅔ cup crème fraîche
225g/8oz cooked chicken, skinned, boned and diced
115g/4oz cooked lean ham, diced
115g/4oz Gouda cheese, grated
15ml/1 tbsp chopped fresh mint
salt and ground black pepper
finely shredded fresh mint, to garnish

1 Cook the pasta in plenty of boiling salted water according to the instructions on the packet.

2 Heat the butter in a large frying pan and fry the onion for about 10 minutes, or until softened.

3 Add the garlic, bay leaf and wine and bring to the boil. Boil rapidly until reduced by about half. Remove the bay leaf, then stir in the crème fraîche and return to the boil.

4 Add the chicken, ham and Gouda cheese and simmer for 5 minutes, stirring occasionally until heated through.

5 Add the chopped fresh mint and season to taste.

6 Drain the pasta thoroughly and turn it into a large serving dish. Toss with the sauce, garnish with finely shredded fresh mint and serve immediately.

Cheesy Pasta Bolognese

Mozzarella gives the cheese sauce a particularly creamy taste.

INGREDIENTS

Serves 4

30ml/2 tbsp olive oil
1 onion, chopped
1 garlic clove, crushed
1 carrot, diced
2 celery sticks, chopped
2 rashers streaky bacon, finely chopped
5 button mushrooms, chopped
450g/1lb lean minced beef
120ml/4fl oz/½ cup red wine
15ml/1 tbsp tomato purée
200g/7oz can chopped tomatoes
fresh thyme sprig
225g/8oz dried penne
300ml/½ pint/1¼ cups milk
25g/1oz/2 tbsp butter
25g/1oz/2 tbsp flour
150g/5oz/1 cup cubed mozzarella cheese
60ml/4 tbsp grated Parmesan cheese
salt and ground black pepper
fresh basil sprigs, to garnish

1 Heat the oil in a pan and fry the onion, garlic, carrot and celery for 6 minutes, until the onions have softened.

2 Add the bacon and continue frying for 3–4 minutes. Stir in the mushrooms, fry for 2 minutes, then add the beef. Fry over a high heat until well browned all over.

3 Pour in the red wine, the tomato purée dissolved in 45ml/3 tbsp water, and the tomatoes, then add the thyme and season well. Bring to the boil, cover the pan and simmer gently for about 30 minutes.

4 Preheat the oven to 200°C/400°F/Gas 6. Bring a pan of water to the boil, add a little oil. Cook the pasta for 10 minutes.

5 Meanwhile, place the milk, butter and flour in a saucepan, heat gently and whisk constantly with a balloon whisk until the mixture is thickened. Stir in the cubed mozzarella cheese, 30ml/2 tbsp of the Parmesan and season lightly.

6 Drain the pasta and stir into the cheese sauce. Uncover the tomato sauce and boil rapidly for about 2 minutes to reduce.

7 Spoon the sauce into an ovenproof dish, top with the pasta mixture and sprinkle the remaining 30ml/2 tbsp Parmesan cheese evenly over the top. Bake for 25 minutes until golden. Garnish with basil and serve hot.

Fusilli with Turkey

Broccoli combines with the other ingredients to make a one-pan meal.

INGREDIENTS

Serves 4

675g/1½lb ripe, firm plum tomatoes, quartered
90ml/6 tbsp olive oil
5ml/1 tsp dried oregano
350g/12oz broccoli florets
1 small onion, sliced
5ml/1 tsp dried thyme
450g/1lb skinless, boneless turkey breast, cubed
3 garlic cloves, crushed
15ml/1 tbsp fresh lemon juice
450g/1lb fusilli
salt and ground black pepper

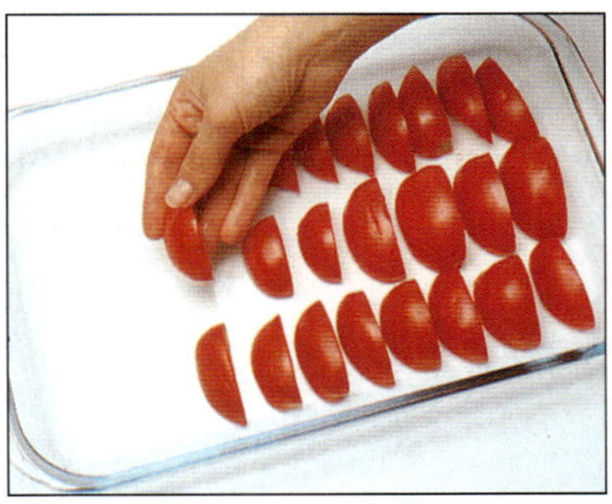

1 Preheat the oven to 200°C/400°F/Gas 6. Place the plum tomatoes in a baking dish. Add 15ml/1 tbsp of the oil, the oregano and 2.5ml/½ tsp salt and stir.

2 Bake for 30–40 minutes, until the tomatoes are just browned; do not stir.

3 Meanwhile, bring a large saucepan of salted water to the boil. Add the broccoli florets and cook until just tender, about 5 minutes. Drain and set aside. (Alternatively, steam the broccoli until tender.)

4 Heat 30ml/2 tbsp of the oil in a large non-stick frying pan. Add the onion, thyme, turkey and 2.5ml/½ tsp salt. Cook over a high heat, stirring often, until the meat is cooked and beginning to brown, about 5–7 minutes. Add the garlic and cook for a further 1 minute, stirring frequently.

5 Remove from the heat. Stir in the lemon juice and season with ground black pepper. Set aside and keep warm.

6 Cook the fusilli in plenty of boiling salted water according to the instructions on the packet until *al dente*. Drain and place in a large bowl. Toss the pasta with the remaining oil.

7 Add the broccoli to the turkey mixture, then stir into the fusilli. Add the tomatoes and stir gently to blend. Serve immediately.

Cheese & Cream Sauces

Tagliatelle with Gorgonzola Sauce

Gorgonzola is a creamy Italian blue cheese. As an alternative you could use Danish Blue or Pipo Creme.

INGREDIENTS

Serves 4

25g/1oz/2 tbsp butter, plus extra for tossing the pasta
225g/8oz Gorgonzola cheese
150ml/¼ pint/⅔ cup double or whipping cream
30ml/2 tbsp dry vermouth
5ml/1 tsp cornflour
15ml/1 tbsp chopped fresh sage
450g/1lb tagliatelle
salt and ground black pepper

1 Melt 25g/1oz/2 tbsp butter in a heavy saucepan (it needs to be thick-based to prevent the cheese from burning). Stir in 175g/6oz crumbled Gorgonzola cheese and stir over a gentle heat for about 2–3 minutes until melted.

2 Whisk in the cream, vermouth and cornflour. Add the sage; season. Cook, whisking, until the sauce boils and thickens. Set aside.

3 Boil the pasta in plenty of salted water according to the instructions on the packet. Drain well and toss with a little butter.

4 Reheat the sauce gently, whisking well. Divide the pasta among four serving bowls, top with the sauce and sprinkle over the remaining crumbled cheese. Serve immediately.

Ravioli with Four-cheese Sauce

This is a smooth, cheesy sauce that coats the pasta very evenly.

INGREDIENTS

Serves 4

350g/12oz ravioli
50g/2oz/¼ cup butter
50g/2oz/¼ cup plain flour
450ml/¾ pint/1¾ cups milk
50g/2oz Parmesan cheese
50g/2oz Edam cheese
50g/2oz Gruyère cheese
50g/2oz fontina cheese
salt and ground black pepper
chopped fresh flat leaf parsley, to garnish

1 Cook the pasta in plenty of boiling salted water according to the instructions on the packet.

2 Melt the butter in a saucepan, stir in the flour and cook for 2 minutes, stirring occasionally.

3 Gradually stir in the milk until completely blended.

4 Bring the milk slowly to the boil, stirring constantly until the sauce is thickened.

5 Grate the cheeses and stir them into the sauce. Stir until they are just beginning to melt. Remove from the heat and season.

6 Drain the pasta thoroughly and turn into a large serving dish. Pour over the sauce and toss to coat. Serve immediately, garnished with the chopped fresh parsley.

Tortellini with Cream, Butter and Cheese

This is an indulgent but quick alternative to macaroni cheese. Stir in some ham or pepperoni if you wish, though it's quite delicious as it is!

INGREDIENTS

Serves 4–6

- 450g/1lb fresh tortellini
- 50g/2oz/4 tbsp butter
- 300ml/½ pint/1¼ cups double cream
- 115g/4oz Parmesan cheese
- freshly grated nutmeg
- salt and ground black pepper

1 Cook the pasta in plenty of boiling salted water according to the instructions on the packet.

2 Meanwhile melt the butter in a medium saucepan and stir in the cream. Bring to the boil and cook for 2–3 minutes until the mixture is slightly thickened.

3 Grate the Parmesan cheese and stir 75g/3oz/¾ cup of it into the sauce until melted. Season to taste with salt, black pepper and nutmeg. Preheat the grill.

4 Drain the pasta well and spoon into a buttered heatproof serving dish. Pour over the sauce, sprinkle over the remaining cheese and place under the grill until brown and bubbling. Serve the tortellini immediately.

Macaroni Cheese with Mushrooms

Macaroni cheese is an all-time classic from the mid-week menu. Here it is served in a light creamy sauce with mushrooms and topped with pine nuts.

INGREDIENTS

Serves 4

450g/1lb quick-cooking elbow macaroni
45ml/3 tbsp olive oil
225g/8oz button mushrooms, sliced
2 fresh thyme sprigs
60ml/4 tbsp plain flour
1 vegetable stock cube
600ml/1 pint/2½ cups milk
2.5ml/½ tsp celery salt
5ml/1 tsp Dijon mustard
175g/6oz/1½ cups grated Cheddar cheese
25g/1oz/¼ cup freshly grated Parmesan cheese
25g/1oz/2 tbsp pine nuts
salt and ground black pepper

1 Cook the macaroni in plenty of boiling salted water according to the instructions on the packet.

COOK'S TIP

Closed button mushrooms are best for white cream sauces. Open varieties can darken a pale sauce to an unattractive sludgy grey.

2 Heat the oil in a heavy-based saucepan. Add the mushrooms and thyme, cover and cook over a gentle heat for 2–3 minutes. Stir in the flour and remove from the heat, add the stock cube and stir continuously until evenly blended. Add the milk, a little at a time, stirring after each addition. Add the celery salt, mustard and Cheddar cheese and season. Stir and simmer for 1–2 minutes until the sauce is thickened.

3 Preheat a moderate grill. Drain the macaroni; toss into the sauce. Turn into four individual dishes or one large flameproof gratin dish. Scatter with grated Parmesan cheese and pine nuts; grill until brown and bubbly.

Pasta with Tomato and Cream Sauce

Here pasta is served with a deliciously rich version of an ordinary tomato sauce.

INGREDIENTS

Serves 4–6

30ml/2 tbsp olive oil
2 garlic cloves, crushed
400g/14oz can chopped tomatoes
150ml/¼ pint/⅔ cup double or whipping cream
30ml/2 tbsp chopped fresh herbs, such as basil, oregano or parsley
450g/1lb pasta, any variety
salt and ground black pepper

1 Heat the oil in a medium saucepan, add the garlic and cook for 2 minutes, until golden.

2 Stir in the tomatoes, bring to the boil and simmer uncovered for 20 minutes, stirring occasionally to prevent sticking. The sauce is ready when you can see the oil separating on top.

3 Add the cream, bring slowly to the boil again and simmer until slightly thickened. Stir in the herbs, taste and season well.

4 Cook the pasta in plenty of boiling salted water according to the instructions on the packet. Drain well and toss with the sauce. Serve piping hot, sprinkled with extra herbs, if you like.

Pasta Twists with Cream and Cheese

Soured cream and two cheeses make a lovely rich sauce.

INGREDIENTS

Serves 4

350g/12oz pasta twists, such as spirali
25g/1oz/2 tbsp butter
1 onion, chopped
1 garlic clove, chopped
15ml/1 tbsp chopped fresh oregano
300ml/½ pint/1¼ cups soured cream
75g/3oz/¾ cup grated mozzarella cheese
75g/3oz/¾ cup grated Bel Paese cheese
5 sun-dried tomatoes in oil, drained and sliced
salt and ground black pepper

1 Cook the pasta in plenty of boiling salted water according to the instructions on the packet.

2 Melt the butter in a large frying pan and fry the onion for about 10 minutes until softened. Add the garlic and cook for 1 minute.

3 Stir in the oregano and cream and heat gently until almost boiling. Stir in the mozzarella and Bel Paese cheese and heat gently, stirring occasionally, until melted. Add the sun-dried tomatoes and season to taste.

4 Drain the pasta twists well and turn into a serving dish. Pour over the sauce and toss well to coat. Serve immediately.

Canneroni with Cheese and Coriander

A speedy supper dish, this is best served with a simple tomato and fresh basil salad.

INGREDIENTS

Serves 4

450g/1lb canneroni
115g/4oz full-fat garlic-and-herb cheese
30ml/2 tbsp very finely chopped fresh coriander
300ml/½ pint/1¼ cups single cream
115g/4oz/1 cup shelled peas, cooked
salt and ground black pepper

1 Cook the pasta in plenty of boiling salted water according to the instructions on the packet.

2 Melt the cheese in a small pan over a low heat until smooth.

3 Stir in the coriander, cream and salt and pepper. Bring slowly to the boil, stirring occasionally, until well blended. Stir in the peas and continue cooking until heated through.

4 Drain the pasta and turn into a large serving dish. Pour over the sauce and toss well to coat thoroughly. Serve immediately.

COOK'S TIP

If you do not like the pronounced flavour of fresh coriander, substitute another fresh herb, such as basil or flat leaf parsley.

Curly Spaghetti with Walnut and Cream

A classic Italian dish with a strong, nutty flavour, this should be served with a delicately flavoured salad.

INGREDIENTS

Serves 4

350g/12oz curly spaghetti (fusilli col buco)
50g/2oz/½ cup walnut pieces
25g/1oz/2 tbsp butter
300ml/½ pint/1¼ cups milk
50g/2oz/1 cup fresh breadcrumbs
25g/1oz/2 tbsp freshly grated Parmesan cheese
pinch of freshly grated nutmeg
salt and ground black pepper
fresh rosemary sprigs, to garnish

1 Cook the pasta in plenty of boiling salted water according to the instructions on the packet. Meanwhile, preheat the grill.

2 Spread the walnuts evenly over the grill pan. Grill for about 5 minutes, turning occasionally until evenly toasted.

3 Remove the walnuts from the heat, place in a clean dish towel and rub away the skins. Roughly chop the nuts.

4 Heat the butter and milk in a saucepan until the butter is completely melted.

5 Stir in the breadcrumbs and nuts and heat gently for 2 minutes, stirring constantly until thickened.

6 Add the Parmesan cheese, nutmeg and seasoning to taste.

7 Drain the pasta thoroughly through a colander and toss in the sauce. Serve immediately, garnished with fresh sprigs of rosemary.

Spaghetti with Feta Cheese

We think of pasta as being essentially Italian but, in fact, the Greeks have a great appetite for it too. It complements tangy, full-flavoured feta cheese beautifully in this simple but effective dish.

INGREDIENTS

Serves 2–3

115g/4oz spaghetti
1 garlic clove
30ml/2 tbsp extra virgin olive oil
8 cherry tomatoes, halved
a little freshly grated nutmeg
salt and ground black pepper
75g/3oz feta cheese, crumbled
15ml/1 tbsp chopped fresh basil
a few black olives, to serve (optional)

1 Cook the spaghetti in plenty of boiling salted water according to the instructions on the packet, then drain well.

2 In the same pan gently heat the garlic clove in the olive oil for 1–2 minutes, then add the halved cherry tomatoes.

3 Increase the heat to fry the tomatoes lightly for 1 minute, then remove the garlic and discard.

4 Toss in the spaghetti, season with the nutmeg and salt and pepper to taste, then stir in the crumbled feta cheese and basil.

5 Check the seasoning, remembering that feta can be quite salty, and serve hot topped with black olives, if desired.

FISH & SHELLFISH SAUCES

Spaghetti with Mixed Shellfish Sauce

A special occasion sauce for an evening of entertaining is just what this is, so serve it in bountiful portions to your guests.

INGREDIENTS

Serves 4

50g/2oz/4 tbsp butter
2 shallots, chopped
2 garlic cloves, chopped
350g/12oz spaghetti
2 tbsp finely chopped fresh basil
300ml/½ pint/1¼ cups dry white wine
450g/1lb mussels, scrubbed
115g/4oz squid, washed
5ml/1 tsp chilli powder
350g/12oz raw peeled prawns
300ml/½ pint/1¼ cups soured cream
salt and ground black pepper
50g/2oz/⅓ cup Parmesan cheese, freshly grated
chopped fresh flat leaf parsley, to garnish

1 Melt half the butter in a frying pan and fry 1 shallot and 1 garlic clove for about 5 minutes until softened.

2 Cook the pasta in plenty of boiling salted water according to the instructions on the packet.

3 Stir in half the basil and the wine and bring to the boil.

4 Discard any mussels that are open and do not shut when tapped with the back of a knife. Quickly add the remaining mussels to the pan, cover and simmer for about 5 minutes until all the shells have opened. Discard any mussels that do not open. Using a slotted spoon, transfer the mussels to a plate, remove them from their shells and return to the pan. Reserve a few mussels in the shells for garnishing.

5 Meanwhile, slice the squid into thin circles. Melt the remaining butter in a frying pan and fry the remaining shallot and garlic for about 5 minutes until softened.

6 Add the remaining basil, the squid, chilli powder and prawns to the pan and stir-fry for 5 minutes until the prawns have turned pink and tender.

7 Turn the mussel mixture into the prawn mixture and bring to the boil. Stir in the soured cream and season to taste. Bring almost to the boil and simmer for 1 minute.

8 Drain the pasta thoroughly and stir it into the sauce with the Parmesan cheese until well coated. Serve immediately, garnished with chopped flat leaf parsley and the reserved mussels in their shells.

Spaghetti with Mussels

Mussels are popular in all the coastal regions of Italy, and are delicious with pasta. This simple dish is greatly improved by using the freshest mussels available.

INGREDIENTS

Serves 4

900g/2lb fresh mussels, in the shell
75ml/5 tbsp olive oil
3 garlic cloves, finely chopped
60ml/4 tbsp chopped fresh parsley
60ml/4 tbsp white wine
400g/14oz spaghetti
salt and ground black pepper

1 Scrub the mussels well under cold running water, carefully cutting off the "beards" with a small sharp knife. Discard any that do not close when tapped sharply.

COOK'S TIP

Mussels should be firmly closed when fresh. If a mussel is slightly open, pinch it closed. If it remains closed on its own, it is alive. If it remains open, discard it. Fresh mussels should be consumed as soon as possible after being purchased. They may be kept in a bowl of cold water in the fridge.

2 Place the mussels with a cupful of water in a large saucepan over a moderate heat. As soon as they open, lift them out one by one with a slotted spoon.

3 When all the mussels have opened (discard any that do not), strain the liquid in the saucepan through a layer of kitchen paper to remove any grit, and reserve until needed.

4 Heat the oil in a large frying pan. Add the garlic and parsley, and cook for 2–3 minutes. Add the mussels, their cooking liquid and the wine. Cook over a moderate heat until heated through.

5 Add a generous amount of pepper to the sauce. Taste for seasoning; add salt if necessary.

6 Cook the pasta in plenty of boiling salted water until *al dente*. Drain, then tip it into the frying pan with the sauce, and stir well over a moderate heat for 3–4 minutes. Serve at once.

Linguine with Clams, Leeks and Tomatoes

Canned clams make this a speedy dish for those in a real hurry.

INGREDIENTS

Serves 4

350g/12oz linguine
25g/1oz/2 tbsp butter
2 leeks, thinly sliced
150ml/¼ pint/⅔ cup dry white wine
4 tomatoes, skinned, seeded and chopped
pinch of turmeric (optional)
250g/9oz can clams, drained
30ml/2 tbsp chopped fresh basil
60ml/4 tbsp crème fraîche
salt and ground black pepper

1 Cook the pasta in plenty of boiling salted water according to the instructions on the packet.

2 Meanwhile, melt the butter in a small saucepan and fry the sliced leeks for about 5 minutes until softened.

3 Add the wine, tomatoes and turmeric, bring to the boil and boil until reduced by half.

4 Stir in the clams, basil, crème fraîche and seasoning and heat through gently without boiling the sauce.

5 Drain the pasta thoroughly and toss in the clam and leek sauce. Serve immediately.

Macaroni with King Prawns and Ham

Cooked radicchio makes a novel addition to this sauce.

INGREDIENTS

Serves 4

350g/12oz short macaroni
45ml/3 tbsp olive oil
12 shelled raw king prawns
1 garlic clove, chopped
175g/6oz/generous 1 cup diced smoked ham
150ml/¼ pint/⅔ cup red wine
½ small radicchio lettuce, shredded
2 egg yolks, beaten
30ml/2 tbsp chopped fresh flat leaf parsley
150ml/¼ pint/⅔ cup double cream
salt and ground black pepper
shredded fresh basil, to garnish

1 Cook the pasta in plenty of boiling salted water, according to the instructions on the packet.

2 Meanwhile, heat the oil in a frying pan and cook the prawns, garlic and ham for about 5 minutes, stirring occasionally until the prawns are tender. Be careful not to overcook.

3 Add the wine and radicchio, bring to the boil and boil rapidly until the juices are reduced by about half.

4 Stir in the egg yolks, parsley and cream and bring almost to the boil, stirring constantly, then simmer until the sauce thickens slightly. Check the seasoning and adjust if necessary.

5 Drain the pasta thoroughly and toss in the sauce to coat. Serve immediately, garnished with some shredded fresh basil.

Spaghetti with Tomato and Clam Sauce

Small sweet clams make this a delicately succulent sauce. Cockles would make a good substitute, or even mussels, but don't be tempted to use seafood pickled in vinegar.

INGREDIENTS

Serves 4

900g/2lb live small clams in the shell, or 2 x 400g/14oz cans clams in brine, drained
90ml/6 tbsp olive oil
2 garlic cloves, crushed
500g/1¼lb canned chopped tomatoes
45ml/3 tbsp chopped fresh parsley
450g/1lb spaghetti
salt and ground black pepper

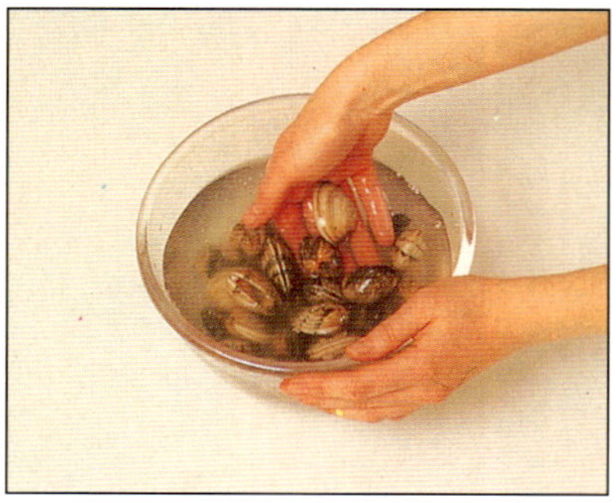

1 If using live clams, place them in a bowl of cold water and rinse several times to remove any grit or sand, then drain well.

2 Heat the oil in a saucepan and add the clams. Stir over a high heat until the clams open. Discard any that do not open. Transfer the clams to a bowl with a slotted spoon and set aside.

3 Reduce the clam juice left in the pan to almost nothing by boiling fast. Add the garlic and fry until golden. Pour in the tomatoes, bring to the boil and cook for 3–4 minutes until reduced. Stir in the clam mixture or canned clams and half the parsley and heat through. Season to taste.

4 Cook the pasta in plenty of boiling salted water according to the instructions on the packet. Drain well and turn into a warm serving dish. Pour over the sauce and sprinkle with the remaining chopped parsley.

Tagliatelle with Haddock and Avocado

You will need to start this recipe the day before because the haddock should be left to marinate overnight.

INGREDIENTS

Serves 4

350g/12oz fresh haddock fillets, skinned
2.5ml/½ tsp each ground cumin, ground coriander and turmeric
150ml/¼ pint/⅔ cup fromage frais
150ml/¼ pint/⅔ cup double cream
15ml/1 tbsp lemon juice
25g/1oz/2 tbsp butter
1 onion, chopped
15ml/1 tbsp plain flour
150ml/¼ pint/⅔ cup fish stock
350g/12oz tagliatelle
1 avocado, peeled, stoned and sliced
2 tomatoes, seeded and chopped
salt and ground black pepper
fresh rosemary sprigs, to garnish

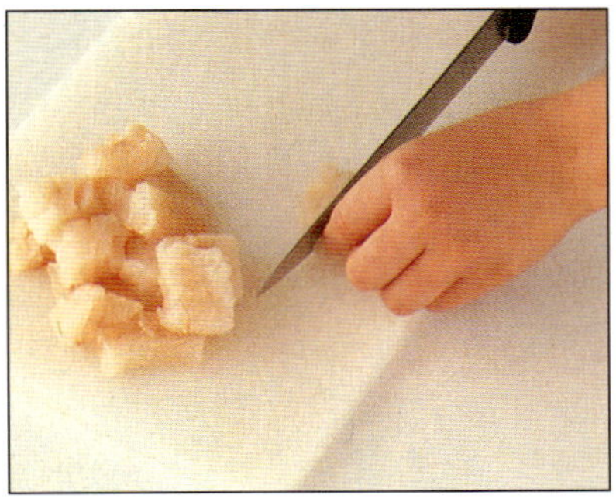

1 Carefully cut the haddock into bite-size pieces.

2 Mix together all the spices, seasoning, fromage frais, cream and lemon juice.

3 Stir in the haddock to coat. Cover the dish and leave to marinate overnight.

4 Heat the butter in a frying pan and fry the onion for about 10 minutes until softened. Stir in the flour, then blend in the stock until smooth.

5 Carefully stir in the haddock mixture until well blended. Bring to the boil, stirring, cover and simmer for about 30 seconds. Remove from the heat.

6 Meanwhile, cook the pasta in plenty of boiling salted water according to the instructions on the packet.

7 Stir the avocado and tomatoes into the haddock mixture.

8 Drain the pasta thoroughly and divide among four serving plates. Spoon over the sauce and serve immediately, garnished with fresh rosemary.

Salmon Pasta with Parsley Sauce

This dish is so quick and easy to make – and delicious.

INGREDIENTS

Serves 4

450g/1lb salmon fillet, skinned
225g/8oz pasta, such as penne or twists
175g/6oz cherry tomatoes, halved
150ml/¼ pint/⅔ cup low -fat crème fraîche
45ml/3 tbsp finely chopped parsley
finely grated rind of ½ orange
salt and ground black pepper

1 Cut the salmon into bite-size pieces, arrange on a heatproof plate and cover with foil.

2 Bring a large pan of salted water to the boil, add the pasta and return to the boil. Place the plate of salmon on top and simmer for 10–12 minutes, until the pasta and salmon are cooked.

3 Drain the pasta and toss with the tomatoes and salmon. Mix together the crème fraîche, parsley, orange rind and pepper to taste, then toss into the salmon and pasta and serve hot or cold.

Pasta with Scallops and Tomato Sauce

Fresh basil gives this sauce a distinctive flavour.

INGREDIENTS

Serves 4

450g/1lb pasta, such as fettucine or linguine
30ml/2 tbsp olive oil
2 garlic cloves, crushed
450g/1lb sea scallops, halved horizontally
salt and ground black pepper
30ml/2 tbsp chopped fresh basil

For the sauce

30ml/2 tbsp olive oil
½ onion, minced
1 garlic clove, crushed
2.5ml/½ tsp salt
2 x 400g/14oz cans plum tomatoes

1 For the sauce, heat the oil in a non-stick frying pan. Add the onion, garlic and a little salt, and cook over a medium heat for about 5 minutes until just softened, stirring occasionally.

2 Add the tomatoes, with their juice, and crush with a fork. Bring to the boil, then reduce the heat and simmer gently for 15 minutes. Remove from the heat and set aside.

3 Cook the pasta in plenty of boiling salted water, according to the instructions on the packet, until *al dente*.

4 Meanwhile, combine the oil and garlic in another non-stick frying pan and cook until just sizzling, about 30 seconds. Add the scallops and 2.5ml/½ tsp salt and cook over a high heat, tossing until the scallops are cooked through, about 3 minutes.

5 Add the scallops to the tomato sauce. Season with salt and pepper, stir and keep warm.

6 Drain the pasta, rinse under hot water and drain again. Place in a large serving dish. Add the sauce and the basil and toss thoroughly. Serve immediately.

Pasta Tubes with Tuna and Olive Sauce

This colourful sauce combines well with a thicker and shorter pasta.

INGREDIENTS

Serves 4

350g/12oz rigatoni
30ml/2 tbsp olive oil
1 onion, chopped
2 garlic cloves, chopped
400g/14oz can chopped tomatoes
50g/2oz/4 tbsp tomato purée
50g/2oz/½ cup stoned black olives, quartered
15ml/1 tbsp chopped fresh oregano
225g/8oz can tuna in oil, drained and flaked
2.5ml/½ tsp anchovy purée
15ml/1 tbsp capers, rinsed
115g/4oz/1 cup grated Cheddar cheese
45ml/3 tbsp fresh white breadcrumbs
salt and ground black pepper
flat leaf parsley sprigs, to garnish

1 Cook the pasta in plenty of boiling salted water according to the instructions on the packet.

2 Meanwhile, heat the oil in a frying pan and fry the onion and garlic for about 10 minutes until softened.

3 Add the tomatoes, tomato purée, and salt and pepper, and bring to the boil. Simmer gently for 5 minutes, stirring occasionally.

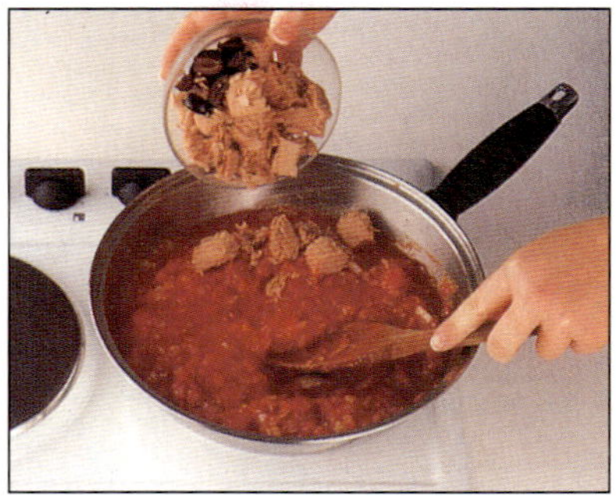

4 Stir in the olives, oregano, tuna, anchovy purée and capers. Spoon the mixture into a mixing bowl.

5 Drain the pasta, toss well in the sauce and spoon into flame-proof serving dishes.

6 Preheat the grill and sprinkle the cheese and breadcrumbs over the pasta. Grill for about 10 minutes until the pasta is heated through and the cheese has melted. Serve at once, garnished with flat leaf parsley.

Tagliatelle with Saffron Mussels

Mussels in a saffron and cream sauce are served with tagliatelle in this recipe, but you can use any other pasta if you prefer.

INGREDIENTS

Serves 4

1.75kg/4–4½lb live mussels in the shell
150ml/¼ pint/⅔ cup dry white wine
2 shallots, chopped
350g/12oz dried tagliatelle
25g/1oz/2 tbsp butter
2 garlic cloves, crushed
250ml/8fl oz/1 cup double cream
generous pinch of saffron strands
1 egg yolk
salt and ground black pepper
30ml/2 tbsp chopped fresh parsley, to garnish

1 Scrub the mussels well under cold running water. Remove the "beards" and discard any mussels that are open.

2 Place the mussels in a large pan with the wine and shallots. Cover and cook over a high heat, shaking the pan occasionally, for 5-8 minutes until the mussels have opened. Drain the mussels, reserving the liquid. Discard any that remain closed. Shell all but a few of the mussels and keep warm.

3 Bring the reserved cooking liquid to the boil, then reduce by half. Strain into a jug to remove any grit.

4 Cook the tagliatelle in plenty of boiling salted water for about 10 minutes, until *al dente*.

5 Meanwhile, melt the butter and fry the garlic for 1 minute. Pour in the mussel liquid, cream and saffron strands. Heat gently until the sauce thickens slightly. Off the heat, stir in the egg yolk, shelled mussels, and season.

6 Drain the tagliatelle and transfer to warmed serving bowls. Spoon the sauce over and sprinkle with chopped parsley. Garnish with the mussels in shells and serve at once.

Seafood Pasta Shells with Spinach Sauce

You'll need very large pasta shells, measuring about 4cm/1½in long for this dish; don't try stuffing smaller shells – they will be much too fiddly!

INGREDIENTS

Serves 4

15g/½oz/1 tbsp margarine
8 spring onions, finely sliced
6 tomatoes
32 large dried pasta shells
225g/8oz/1 cup low-fat soft cheese
90ml/6 tbsp skimmed milk
pinch of freshly grated nutmeg
225g/8oz/2 cups prawns
175g/6oz can white crab meat, drained and flaked
115g/4oz frozen chopped spinach, thawed and drained
salt and ground black pepper

1 Preheat the oven to 150°C/300°F/Gas 2. Melt the margarine in a small saucepan and gently cook the spring onions for 3–4 minutes, or until softened.

2 Slash the bottoms of the tomatoes, plunge into a saucepan of boiling water for 45 seconds, then into a saucepan of cold water. Slip off the skins. Halve the tomatoes, remove the seeds and cores and roughly chop the flesh.

3 Cook the pasta shells in plenty of boiling salted water for about 10 minutes, or until *al dente*. Drain well.

4 Heat the soft cheese and milk in a saucepan, stirring until blended. Season with salt, pepper and nutmeg. Measure 30ml/2 tbsp of the sauce into a bowl.

5 Add the spring onions, tomatoes, prawns, and crab meat to the bowl. Mix well. Spoon the filling into the shells and place in a single layer in a shallow ovenproof dish. Cover with foil and cook in the preheated oven for 10 minutes.

6 Stir the spinach into the remaining sauce. Bring to the boil and simmer gently for 1 minute, stirring all the time. Drizzle over the pasta shells and serve hot.

Spaghetti with Seafood Sauce

The Italian name for this tomato-based sauce is marinara.

INGREDIENTS

Serves 4

45ml/3 tbsp olive oil
1 onion, chopped
1 garlic clove, finely chopped
225g/8oz spaghetti
600ml/1 pint/2½ cups passata
15ml/1 tbsp tomato purée
5ml/1 tsp dried oregano
1 bay leaf
5ml/1 tsp sugar
115g/4oz/1 cup cooked peeled shrimps (rinsed well if canned)
115g/4oz/1 cup cooked peeled prawns
175g/6oz/1½ cups cooked clam or cockle meat (rinsed well if canned or bottled)
15ml/1 tbsp lemon juice
45ml/3 tbsp chopped fresh parsley
25g/1oz/2 tbsp butter
salt and ground black pepper
4 whole cooked prawns, to garnish

1 Heat the oil in a pan and add the onion and garlic. Fry over a moderate heat for 6–7 minutes, until the onions have softened.

2 Meanwhile, cook the spaghetti in a large saucepan of boiling salted water for 10–12 minutes until *al dente.*

3 Stir the passata, tomato purée, oregano, bay leaf and sugar into the onions and season well. Bring to the boil, then simmer for 2–3 minutes.

4 Add the shellfish, lemon juice and 30ml/2 tbsp of the parsley. Stir well, then cover and cook for 6–7 minutes.

5 Meanwhile, drain the spaghetti when it is ready and add the butter to the pan. Return the drained spaghetti to the pan and toss in the butter. Season well.

6 Divide the spaghetti among four warmed plates and top with the seafood sauce. Sprinkle with the remaining chopped parsley, garnish with whole prawns and serve immediately.

Pasta with Fresh Sardine Sauce

In this classic Sicilian dish, fresh sardines are combined with raisins and pine nuts.

INGREDIENTS

Serves 4

30g/1¼oz/3 tbsp sultanas
450g/1lb fresh sardines
90ml/6 tbsp breadcrumbs
1 small fennel bulb
90ml/6 tbsp olive oil
1 onion, very thinly sliced
30g/1¼oz/3 tbsp pine nuts
2.5ml/½ tsp fennel seeds
400g/14oz long hollow pasta, such as percatelli, zite or bucatini
salt and ground black pepper

1 Soak the sultanas in warm water for 15 minutes. Drain and pat dry.

2 Clean the sardines. Open each one out flat and remove the central bones and head. Wash well and shake dry. Sprinkle evenly with the breadcrumbs.

3 Coarsely chop the top fronds of fennel and reserve. Pull off a few outer leaves and wash. Fill a large saucepan with enough water to cook the pasta. Add the fennel leaves and bring to the boil.

4 Heat the oil in a large frying pan and sauté the onion lightly until soft. Remove to a side dish. Add the sardines, a few at a time, and cook over a moderate heat until golden on both sides, turning once. When all the sardines have been cooked, gently return them to the pan. Add the onion, and the sultanas, pine nuts and fennel seeds. Season with salt and pepper.

5 Take about 60ml/4 tbsp of the boiling water for the pasta, and add it to the sauce. Add salt to the boiling water, and cook the pasta until *al dente*. Drain, and remove the fennel leaves. Dress the pasta with the sauce. Divide among four individual serving plates, arranging several sardines on each. Sprinkle with the reserved chopped fennel tops and serve at once.

Pasta with Spinach and Anchovy Sauce

Deliciously earthy, this would make a good starter or light supper dish. Add some sultanas to the sauce to ring the changes.

INGREDIENTS

Serves 4

900g/2lb fresh spinach or 500g/1¼lb frozen leaf spinach, thawed
450g/1lb angel hair pasta
salt, to taste
60ml/4 tbsp olive oil
45ml/3 tbsp pine nuts
2 garlic cloves
6 canned anchovy fillets, drained and chopped, or whole salted anchovies, rinsed, boned and chopped
butter, for tossing the pasta

1 If using fresh spinach, wash it well and remove any tough stalks. Drain thoroughly. Place in a large saucepan with only the water that clings to the leaves. Cover with a lid and cook over a high heat, shaking the pan occasionally, until the spinach is just wilted and still bright green. Drain.

2 Cook the pasta in plenty of boiling salted water according to the instructions on the packet.

3 Heat the oil in a saucepan and fry the pine nuts until golden. Remove with a slotted spoon. Add the garlic to the oil in the pan and fry until golden. Add the chopped anchovies to the pan.

4 Stir in the spinach and cook for 2–3 minutes or until heated through. Stir in the pine nuts. Drain the pasta, toss in a little butter and turn into a warmed serving dish. Top with the hot sauce and fork through roughly before serving.

Rigatoni with Scallop Sauce

A jewel from the sea, the scallop is what makes this sauce so special. Serve with a green salad, if liked.

INGREDIENTS

Serves 4

350g/12oz rigatoni
350g/12oz queen scallops
45ml/3 tbsp olive oil
1 garlic clove, chopped
1 onion, chopped
2 carrots, cut into matchsticks
30 ml/2 tbsp chopped fresh parsley
30ml/2 tbsp dry white wine
30ml/2 tbsp Pernod
150ml/¼ pint/⅔ cup double cream
salt and ground black pepper

1 Cook the pasta in plenty of boiling salted water according to the instructions on the packet.

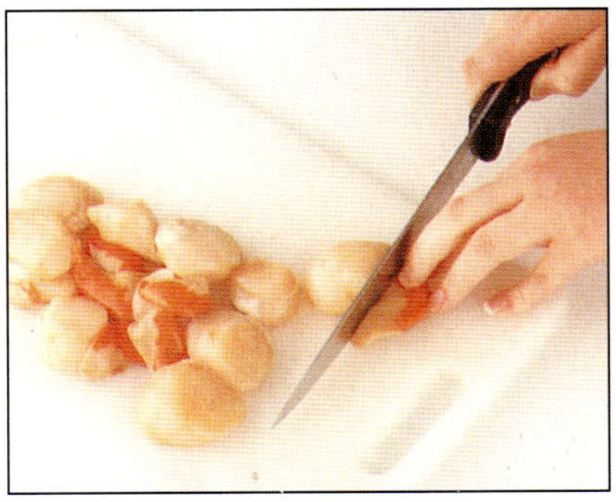

2 Trim the scallops, separating the corals from the white eye part of the meat.

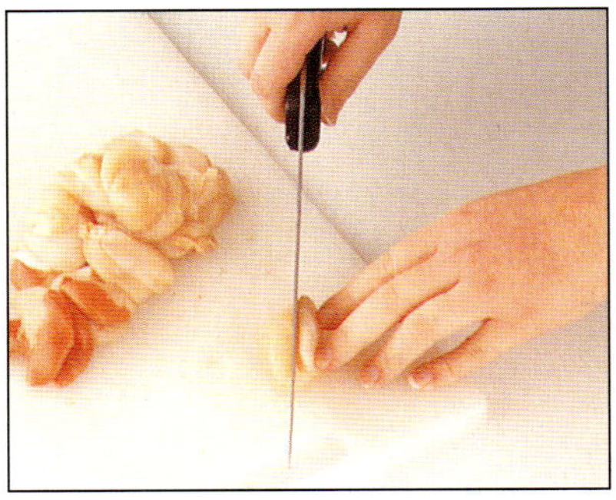

3 Using a sharp knife, cut the eye in half lengthways.

4 Heat the oil in a frying pan and fry the garlic, onion and carrots for 5–10 minutes until the carrots are softened.

5 Stir in the scallops, parsley, wine and Pernod and bring to the boil. Cover and simmer for about 1 minute. Using a slotted spoon, transfer the scallops and vegetables to a plate and keep them warm until required.

6 Bring the pan juices back to the boil and boil rapidly until reduced by half. Stir in the cream and heat the sauce through.

7 Return the scallops and vegetables to the pan and heat them through. Season to taste.

8 Drain the pasta thoroughly and toss with the sauce. Serve the rigatoni immediately.

Fusilli with Vegetable and Prawn Sauce

You will need to start this recipe the day before because the prawns should be left to marinate overnight.

INGREDIENTS

Serves 4

450g/1lb/4 cups peeled prawns
60ml/4 tbsp soy sauce
45ml/3 tbsp olive oil
350g/12oz curly spaghetti (fusilli col buco)
1 yellow pepper, cored, seeded and cut into strips
225g/8oz broccoli florets
1 bunch spring onions, shredded
2.5cm/1in piece fresh ginger root, peeled and shredded
15ml/1 tbsp chopped fresh oregano
30ml/2 tbsp dry sherry
15ml/1 tbsp cornflour
300ml/½ pint/1¼ cups fish stock
salt and ground black pepper

1 Place the prawns in a mixing bowl. Stir in half the soy sauce and 30ml/2 tbsp of the olive oil. Cover and marinate overnight.

2 Cook the pasta in plenty of boiling salted water according to the instructions on the packet.

3 Meanwhile, heat the remaining oil in a wok or frying pan and fry the prawns for 1 minute.

4 Add the pepper, broccoli, spring onions, ginger and oregano and stir-fry for about 1–2 minutes.

5 Drain the pasta thoroughly, set aside and keep warm. Meanwhile, blend together the sherry and cornflour until smooth. Stir in the stock and remaining soy sauce until well blended.

6 Pour the sauce into the wok or pan, bring to the boil and stir-fry for 2 minutes until thickened. Pour over the pasta and serve.

Mixed Summer Pasta

A pretty and colourful sauce with bags of flavour makes this a popular dish for the summer.

INGREDIENTS

Serves 4

115g/4oz French beans, cut into 2.5cm/1in pieces
350g/12oz curly spaghetti (fusilli col buco)
30ml/2 tbsp olive oil
½ fennel bulb, sliced
1 bunch spring onions, sliced diagonally
115g/4oz yellow cherry tomatoes
115g/4oz red cherry tomatoes
30ml/2 tbsp chopped fresh dill
225g/8oz/2 cups peeled prawns
15ml/1 tbsp lemon juice
15ml/1 tbsp wholegrain mustard
60ml/4 tbsp soured cream
salt and ground black pepper
fresh dill sprigs, to garnish

1 Cook the beans in a saucepan of boiling salted water for about 5 minutes until tender. Drain through a colander.

2 Cook the pasta in plenty of boiling salted water, according to the instructions on the packet, until *al dente*.

3 Heat the oil in a frying pan and fry the sliced fennel and spring onions for about 5 minutes.

4 Stir in all the cherry tomatoes and fry for a further 5 minutes, stirring occasionally.

5 Add the dill and prawns and cook for 1 minute.

6 Stir in the lemon juice, wholegrain mustard, soured cream, seasoning and beans and simmer for 1 minute.

7 Drain the pasta and toss with the sauce. Serve immediately, garnished with fresh dill.

VEGETABLE SAUCES

Pasta Napoletana

The simple classic cooked tomato sauce with no adornments.

INGREDIENTS

Serves 4

900g/2lb fresh ripe red tomatoes or 750g/1¾lb canned plum tomatoes with their juice
1 onion, chopped
1 carrot, diced
1 celery stick, diced
150ml/¼ pint/⅔ cup dry white wine (optional)
1 sprig fresh parsley
pinch of caster sugar
15ml/1 tbsp chopped fresh oregano or 5ml/1 tsp dried
450g/1lb pasta, any variety
salt and ground black pepper
freshly grated Parmesan cheese, to serve

1 Roughly chop the tomatoes and place in a medium saucepan.

2 Add all the other ingredients, except the oregano, pasta and cheese, and bring to the boil. Simmer, half-covered, for about 45 minutes until very thick, stirring occasionally. Strain, then stir in the oregano. Taste and adjust the seasoning if necessary.

3 Cook the pasta in plenty of boiling salted water according to the instructions on the packet, until *al dente*. Drain well.

4 Toss the pasta with the sauce. Serve with plenty of freshly grated Parmesan cheese.

Spaghetti with Herb Sauce

Herbs make a wonderfully aromatic sauce – the heat from the pasta releases their flavours.

INGREDIENTS

Serves 4

50g/2oz chopped fresh mixed herbs, such as parsley, basil and thyme
2 garlic cloves, crushed
60ml/4 tbsp pine nuts, toasted
150ml/¼ pint/⅔ cup olive oil
350g/12oz dried spaghetti
60ml/4 tbsp freshly grated Parmesan cheese
salt and ground black pepper
basil leaves, to garnish

1 Put the herbs, garlic and half the pine nuts into a blender or food processor. With the machine running slowly, add the oil and process to form a thick purée.

2 Cook the spaghetti in plenty of boiling salted water for about 8 minutes until *al dente*. Drain.

3 Transfer the herb purée to a large warmed serving dish, then add the spaghetti and Parmesan. Toss well to coat the pasta with the sauce. Sprinkle over the remaining pine nuts and the basil leaves and serve immediately.

Pasta with Courgette and Walnut Sauce

The vegetables are softened slowly to release their flavours.

INGREDIENTS

Serves 4

65g/2½oz/5 tbsp butter
1 large Spanish onion, halved and thinly sliced
450g/1lb courgettes, very thinly sliced
375g/12oz short pasta shapes, such as penne, ziti, rotini or fusilli
50g/2oz/½ cup walnuts, coarsely chopped
45ml/3 tbsp chopped fresh parsley
30ml/2 tbsp single cream
salt and ground black pepper
freshly grated Parmesan cheese, to serve

1 Melt the butter in a frying pan. Add the onion, cover and sweat for 5 minutes until translucent, then add the courgettes.

2 Stir well, cover again and sweat until the vegetables are very soft, stirring occasionally.

3 Meanwhile, cook the pasta in plenty of boiling salted water, according to the instructions on the packet, until *al dente*.

4 While the pasta is cooking, add the walnuts, parsley and cream to the courgette mixture and stir well. Season with salt and pepper.

5 Drain the pasta and return to the pan. Add the courgette sauce and mix together well. Serve immediately, with freshly grated Parmesan to sprinkle over.

Tagliatelle with Sun-dried Tomatoes

Choose plain sun-dried tomatoes for this sauce, instead of those preserved in oil, if you wish to reduce the fat content of the dish.

INGREDIENTS

Serves 4

1 garlic clove, crushed
1 celery stick, finely sliced
115g/4oz/1 cup sun-dried tomatoes, finely chopped
90ml/3½fl oz/scant ½ cup red wine
8 plum tomatoes
350g/12oz dried tagliatelle
salt and ground black pepper

1 Put the garlic, celery, sun-dried tomatoes and wine into a large saucepan. Gently cook for about 15 minutes.

2 Slash the bottoms of the plum tomatoes and plunge into a saucepan of boiling water for 1 minute, then into a saucepan of cold water. Slip off their skins. Halve, remove the seeds and cores and roughly chop the flesh.

3 Add the plum tomatoes to the saucepan and simmer for a further 5 minutes. Season to taste.

4 Meanwhile, cook the tagliatelle in plenty of boiling salted water for 8–10 minutes, or until *al dente*. Drain well. Toss with half the sauce and serve on warmed plates, with the remaining sauce.

Macaroni with Hazelnut and Coriander Sauce

This is a variation on pesto sauce, giving a smooth, herby flavour of coriander.

INGREDIENTS

Serves 4

350g/12oz macaroni
50g/2oz/⅓ cup hazelnuts
2 garlic cloves
1 bunch fresh coriander
1 tsp salt
90ml/6 tbsp olive oil
fresh coriander sprigs, to garnish

1 Cook the pasta following the instructions on the packet, until *al dente*.

2 Meanwhile, finely chop the hazelnuts.

3 Place the nuts and remaining ingredients, except 1 tbsp of the oil, in a food processor, or use a pestle and mortar and grind together to create the sauce.

4 Heat the remaining oil in a saucepan and add the sauce. Fry very gently for about 1 minute until heated through.

5 Drain the pasta thoroughly and stir it into the sauce. Toss well to coat. Serve immediately, garnished with fresh coriander.

COOK'S TIP

To remove the skins from the hazelnuts, place them in a 180°C/350°F/Gas 4 oven for 20 minutes, then rub off the skins with a clean dish towel.

Spaghetti with Aubergine and Tomato

A great supper recipe – serve this aubergine and tomato dish with freshly cooked mange-touts.

INGREDIENTS

Serves 4

3 small aubergines
olive oil, for frying
450g/1lb spaghetti
1 quantity Classic Tomato Sauce (see Curly Lasagne with Classic Tomato Sauce)
225g/8oz fontina cheese, grated
salt and ground black pepper

1 Top and tail the aubergines and slice thinly. Arrange in a colander, sprinkling with plenty of salt between each layer. Leave to stand for about 30 minutes.

2 Rinse the aubergines under cold running water. Drain and pat dry on kitchen paper.

3 Heat plenty of oil in a large frying pan and fry the aubergine slices in batches for about 5 minutes, turning them once during the cooking time, until evenly browned.

4 Meanwhile, cook the pasta in plenty of boiling salted water according to the instructions on the packet, until *al dente*.

5 Stir the tomato sauce into the pan with the aubergines and bring to the boil. Cover and then simmer for 5 minutes.

6 Stir in the fontina cheese and salt and pepper. Continue stirring over a medium heat until the cheese melts.

7 Drain the pasta and stir into the sauce, tossing well to coat. Serve immediately.

Pasta Spirals with Pesto Sauce

A light, fragrant sauce like this dish gives a temptingly different taste.

INGREDIENTS

Serves 4

350g/12oz pasta spirals (fusilli)
50g/2oz fresh basil leaves, without the stalks
2 garlic cloves, chopped
30ml/2 tbsp pine nuts
salt and freshly ground black pepper
150ml/¼ pint/⅔ cup olive oil
50g/2oz/⅓ cup Parmesan cheese, freshly grated, plus extra to garnish
fresh basil sprigs, to garnish

COOK'S TIP

Fresh basil is widely available from most greengrocers and supermarkets, either in growing pots or packets. If you buy a plant, remove the flowers as they appear so the plant grows more leaves.

Pesto is best kept in a screw-topped jar in the fridge for up to two days. If you want to keep it a few days longer, cover the top with a thin layer of olive oil. This can be stirred into the sauce when you are ready to add it to hot pasta.

1 Cook the pasta following the instructions on the packet until *al dente*.

2 To make the pesto sauce, place the basil leaves, garlic, pine nuts, seasoning and olive oil in a food processor or blender. Blend until very creamy.

3 Transfer the mixture to a bowl and stir in the freshly grated Parmesan cheese.

4 Drain the pasta thoroughly and turn it into a large bowl. Pour the sauce over and toss to coat. Divide among serving plates and serve, sprinkled with the extra Parmesan cheese and garnished with fresh basil sprigs.

Lasagne Rolls

Perhaps a more elegant presentation than ordinary lasagne, but just as tasty and popular. You will need to boil "no-need-to-cook" lasagne as it needs to be soft enough to roll!

INGREDIENTS

Serves 4

8-10 lasagne sheets
225g/8oz fresh leaf spinach, well washed
115g/4oz mushrooms, sliced
115g/4oz mozzarella cheese, thinly sliced
Lentil Bolognese (see below)

Béchamel Sauce

50g/2oz/scant ½ cup all-purpose flour
45ml/3 tbsp butter or margarine
600ml/1 pint/2½ cups milk
bay leaf
salt and ground black pepper
freshly grated nutmeg
freshly grated Parmesan or pecorino cheese, to serve

1 Cook the lasagne sheets according to instructions on the package, or until *al dente*. Drain and allow to cool.

2 Cook the spinach in the tiniest amount of water for 2 minutes then add the sliced mushrooms and cook for a further 2 minutes. Drain very well, pressing out all the excess liquor, and chop the spinach roughly.

3 Put all the béchamel ingredients into a saucepan and bring slowly to a boil, stirring until the sauce is thick and smooth. Simmer for 2 minutes with the bay leaf, then season well and stir in the grated nutmeg to taste.

4 Lay out the pasta sheets and spread with the béchamel sauce, spinach, mushrooms and mozzarella. Roll up each one and place in a large shallow casserole dish with the join face down in the dish.

5 Remove and discard the bay leaf and then pour the sauce over the pasta. Sprinkle the cheese and place under a hot grill to brown.

VARIATION

Needless to say, the fillings in this recipe could be any of your own choice. Another favourite is a lightly stir-fried mixture of colourful vegetables such as peppers, courgettes, aubergines and mushrooms, topped with a cheese béchamel as above, or with a fresh tomato sauce, which is especially good in summer.

Lentil Bolognese

A really useful sauce to serve with pasta, such as Lasagne Rolls (as above), as a crêpe stuffing or even as a protein-packed sauce for vegetables.

INGREDIENTS

Serves 6

1 onion
2 garlic cloves, crushed
2 carrots, coarsely grated
2 celery stalks, chopped
45ml/3 tbsp olive oil
150g/5oz/⅔ cup red lentils
14 oz can chopped tomatoes
45ml/3 tbsp tomato paste
475ml/16fl oz/2 cups stock
15ml/1 tbsp fresh marjoram, chopped, or 5ml/1 tsp dried marjoram
salt and ground black pepper

1 In a large saucepan, gently fry the onion, garlic, carrots and celery in the oil for about 5 minutes, until they are soft.

2 Add the lentils, tomatoes, tomato paste, stock and marjoram, and season to taste.

3 Bring the mixture to a boil, then partially cover with a lid and simmer for 20 minutes until thick and soft. Use the bolognese sauce as required.

Pasta with Spring Vegetables

Don't be tempted to use dried herbs in this flavoursome dish.

INGREDIENTS

Serves 4

115g/4oz broccoli florets
115g/4oz baby leeks
225g/8oz asparagus
1 small fennel bulb
115g/4oz/1 cup fresh or frozen peas
40g/1½oz/3 tbsp butter
1 shallot, chopped
45ml/3 tbsp chopped fresh mixed herbs, such as parsley, thyme and sage
300ml/½ pint/1¼ cups double cream
350g/12oz dried penne
salt and ground black pepper
freshly grated Parmesan cheese, to serve

1 Divide the broccoli florets into tiny sprigs. Cut the leeks and asparagus diagonally into 5cm/2in lengths. Trim the fennel bulb and remove any tough outer leaves. Cut into wedges, leaving the layers attached at the root ends so the pieces stay intact.

2 Cook each vegetable, including the peas, separately in boiling salted water until just tender – use the same water for each vegetable. Drain well and keep warm.

3 Melt the butter in a separate pan, add the chopped shallot and cook, stirring occasionally, until softened but not browned. Stir in the herbs and cream and cook for a few minutes, until slightly thickened.

4 Meanwhile, cook the pasta in plenty of boiling salted water for 10 minutes until *al dente*. Drain well and add to the sauce with the vegetables. Toss gently and season with plenty of pepper.

5 Serve the pasta hot with a sprinkling of freshly grated Parmesan cheese.

Spaghetti with Olives and Mushrooms

A rich, pungent sauce topped with sweet cherry tomatoes.

INGREDIENTS

Serves 4

15ml/1 tbsp olive oil
1 garlic clove, chopped
225g/8oz mushrooms, chopped
150g/5oz/scant 1 cup black olives, stoned
30ml/2 tbsp chopped fresh parsley
1 red chilli, seeded and chopped
450g/1lb spaghetti
225g/8oz cherry tomatoes
Parmesan cheese shavings, to serve (optional)

1 Heat the oil in a large pan. Add the garlic; cook for 1 minute. Add the chopped mushrooms, cover, and cook over a medium heat for 5 minutes.

2 Place the mushrooms in a blender or food processor with the olives, parsley and red chilli. Blend until smooth.

3 Cook the pasta in plenty of boiling salted water, according to the instructions on the packet, until *al dente*. Drain well and return to the pan. Add the olive mixture and toss together until the pasta is well coated. Cover and keep warm.

4 Heat an ungreased frying pan and shake the cherry tomatoes around until they start to split, about 2–3 minutes. Serve the pasta topped with the tomatoes and garnished with Parmesan cheese shavings, if desired.

Spaghetti with Garlic and Oil

This is one of the simplest and most satisfying pasta dishes of all. It is very popular throughout Italy. Use the best quality oil available for this splendid dish.

INGREDIENTS

Serves 4

400g/14oz spaghetti
90ml/6 tbsp extra virgin olive oil
3 garlic cloves, chopped
60ml/4 tbsp chopped fresh parsley
salt and ground black pepper
freshly grated Parmesan cheese, to serve (optional)

1 Cook the spaghetti in plenty of boiling salted water.

2 In a large frying pan heat the oil and gently sauté the garlic until barely golden. Do not let it brown or it will taste bitter. Stir in the chopped fresh parsley, then season with salt and pepper. Remove from the heat until the pasta is ready.

3 Drain the pasta when it is barely *al dente*. Tip it into the pan with the oil and garlic, and cook together for 2–3 minutes, stirring well to coat the spaghetti with the sauce. Serve at once in a warmed serving bowl, with some Parmesan cheese, if desired.

Spaghetti with Walnut Sauce

Like pesto, this sauce is traditionally ground in a pestle and mortar , but works just as well made in a blender or food processor. It is also good on tagliatelle and other pasta noodles.

INGREDIENTS

Serves 4

115g/4oz/1 cup walnut pieces or halves
45ml/3 tbsp plain breadcrumbs
45ml/3 tbsp olive or walnut oil
45ml/3 tbsp chopped fresh parsley
1–2 garlic cloves (optional)
50g/2oz/¼ cup butter, at room temperature
30ml/2 tbsp double cream
400g/14oz wholemeal spaghetti
salt and ground black pepper
freshly grated Parmesan cheese, to serve

1 Drop the nuts into a small pan of boiling water, and cook for 1–2 minutes. Drain, then skin. Dry on kitchen paper. Coarsely chop and set aside about a quarter.

2 Place the remaining nuts, the breadcrumbs, oil, parsley and garlic, if using, in a blender or food processor. Process to a paste. Remove to a bowl, and stir in the softened butter and the cream. Season with salt and pepper.

3 Cook the pasta in plenty of boiling salted water, following the instructions on the packet, until *al dente*. Drain, then toss with the sauce. Sprinkle with the reserved chopped nuts, and hand round the grated Parmesan separately.

Campanelle with Yellow Pepper Sauce

Roasted yellow peppers make a deliciously sweet and creamy sauce to serve with pasta.

INGREDIENTS

Serves 4

2 yellow peppers
50g/2oz/¼ cup soft goat's cheese
115g/4oz/½ cup low-fat fromage blanc
450g/1lb short pasta, such as campanelle or fusilli
salt and ground black pepper
50g/2oz/½ cup toasted flaked almonds, to serve

1 Place the whole yellow peppers under a preheated grill until charred and blistered. Place in a plastic bag, seal and leave to cool. Then peel and remove all the seeds.

2 Place the pepper flesh in a blender or food processor with the goat's cheese and fromage blanc. Process until smooth. Season with salt and plenty of ground black pepper.

3 Cook the pasta in plenty of boiling salted water, according to the instructions on the packet, until *al dente*. Drain well.

4 Toss with the sauce and serve sprinkled with the toasted flaked almonds.

Tagliatelle with Walnut Sauce

An unusual sauce which would make this a spectacular dinner party starter or satisfying supper.

INGREDIENTS

Serves 4–6

2 thick slices wholemeal bread
300ml/½ pint/1¼ cups milk
275g/10oz/2½ cups walnut pieces
1 garlic clove, crushed
50g/2oz/½ cup freshly grated Parmesan cheese
90ml/6 tbsp olive oil, plus extra for tossing the pasta
150ml/¼ pint/⅔ cup double cream (optional)
450g/1lb tagliatelle
salt and ground black pepper
30ml/2 tbsp chopped fresh parsley, to garnish

1 Cut the crusts off the bread and soak in the milk until all of the milk is absorbed.

2 Preheat the oven to 190°C/375°F/Gas 5. Spread the walnuts on a baking sheet and toast in the oven for 5 minutes. Leave to cool.

3 Place the bread, walnuts, garlic, Parmesan cheese and olive oil in a blender or food processor and blend until smooth. Season to taste with salt and pepper. Stir in the cream, if using.

4 Cook the pasta in plenty of boiling salted water according to the instructions on the packet, drain and toss with a little olive oil. Divide the pasta equally among four or six bowls and place a dollop of sauce on each portion. Sprinkle with parsley.

Basic Tomato Sauce

Tomato sauce is without doubt the most popular dressing for pasta in Italy. This sauce is best made with fresh tomatoes, but works well with canned plum tomatoes.

INGREDIENTS

Serves 4

60ml/4 tbsp olive oil
1 onion, very finely chopped
1 garlic clove, finely chopped
450g/1lb tomatoes, fresh or canned, chopped with their juice
a few fresh basil leaves or parsley sprigs
salt and ground black pepper

1 Heat the oil in a medium saucepan. Add the onion, and cook over a moderate heat until it is translucent, 5–8 minutes.

2 Stir in the garlic and the tomatoes with their juice (add 45ml/3 tbsp of water if you are using fresh tomatoes). Season with salt and pepper. Add the herbs. Cook for 20–30 minutes.

3 Pass the sauce through a food mill or purée in a blender or food processor. To serve, reheat gently, correct the seasoning and pour over drained pasta.

Special Tomato Sauce

The tomatoes in this sauce are enhanced by the addition of extra vegetables. It is good served with all types of pasta.

INGREDIENTS

Serves 6

700g/1⅔lb tomatoes, fresh or canned, chopped
1 carrot, chopped
1 celery stick, chopped
1 onion, chopped
1 garlic clove, crushed
75ml/5 tbsp olive oil
a few fresh basil leaves or small pinch dried oregano
salt and ground black pepper

1 Place all the ingredients in a medium heavy saucepan, and simmer for 30 minutes.

2 Purée the sauce in a blender or food processor; alternatively press through a sieve.

COOK'S TIP

This sauce may be spooned into freezer bags and frozen until required. Allow to thaw at room temperature before reheating.

3 Return the sauce to the pan, correct the seasoning, and bring to a simmer. Cook for about 15 minutes, then pour over drained cooked pasta.

Spaghetti with Olives and Capers

This spicy sauce originated in the Naples area. It can be quickly assembled using a few store-cupboard ingredients.

INGREDIENTS

Serves 4

60ml/4 tbsp olive oil
2 garlic cloves, finely chopped
small piece of dried red chilli, crumbled
50g/2oz can anchovy fillets, chopped
350g/12oz tomatoes, fresh or canned, chopped
115g/4oz/1 cup stoned black olives
30ml/2 tbsp capers, rinsed
15ml/1 tbsp tomato purée
400g/14oz spaghetti
30ml/2 tbsp chopped fresh parsley

1 Heat the oil in a large frying pan. Add the garlic and the dried red chilli, and cook for 2–3 minutes until the garlic is just golden.

2 Add the chopped anchovies, and mash them into the garlic with a fork.

3 Add the fresh or canned tomatoes, olives, capers and tomato purée. Stir well and cook over a moderate heat.

4 Cook the spaghetti in plenty of boiling salted water until *al dente*. Drain well.

5 Turn the spaghetti into the sauce. Increase the heat and cook for 3–4 minutes, turning the pasta constantly. Sprinkle with parsley and serve at once.

Pasta Spirals with Lentils and Cheese

This surprising combination works extremely well.

INGREDIENTS

Serves 4

15ml/1 tbsp olive oil
1 onion, chopped
1 garlic clove, chopped
1 carrot, cut into matchsticks
350g/12oz pasta spirals, such as fusilli
65g/2½oz/½ cup green lentils, boiled for 25 minutes
15ml/1 tbsp tomato purée
15ml/1 tbsp chopped fresh oregano
150ml/¼ pint/⅔ cup vegetable stock
225g/8oz/2 cups grated Cheddar cheese
salt and ground black pepper
freshly grated cheese, to serve

1 Heat the oil in a large frying pan and fry the onion and garlic for 3 minutes. Add the carrot and cook for a further 5 minutes.

2 Cook the pasta in plenty of boiling salted water according to the instructions on the packet.

3 Add the lentils, tomato purée and oregano to the frying pan, stir, cover and cook for 3 minutes.

4 Add the stock and salt and pepper to the pan. Cover and simmer for 10 minutes. Add the grated Cheddar cheese.

5 Drain the pasta thoroughly and stir into the sauce to coat. Serve with plenty of extra grated cheese.

COOK'S TIP

Tomato purée is sold in small cans and tubes. If you use a can for this small amount, you can keep the remainder fresh by transferring it to a bowl, covering it with a thin layer of olive oil and putting it in the fridge until needed.

Greek Pasta with Avocado Sauce

This is an unusual sauce with a pale green colour, studded with red tomato. It has a luxurious, velvety texture. The sauce is rather rich, so you don't need too much of it.

INGREDIENTS

Serves 6

3 ripe tomatoes
2 large ripe avocados
25g/1oz/2 tbsp butter, plus extra for tossing the pasta
1 garlic clove, crushed
350ml/12fl oz/1½ cups double cream
dash of Tabasco sauce
450g/1lb green tagliatelle
salt and ground black pepper
freshly grated Parmesan cheese, to garnish
60ml/4 tbsp soured cream, to garnish

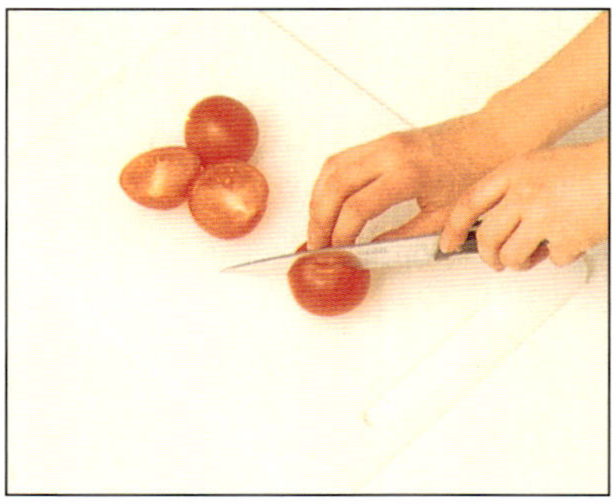

1 Halve the tomatoes and remove the cores. Squeeze out the seeds and dice the flesh. Set aside until required.

2 Halve the avocados, remove the stones and peel. Roughly chop the flesh. If hard-skinned, scoop out the flesh with a spoon.

3 Melt the butter in a saucepan and add the garlic. Cook for 1 minute, then add the cream and chopped avocados. Increase the heat, stirring constantly to break up the avocados.

4 Add the diced tomatoes and season to taste with salt, pepper and a little Tabasco sauce. Keep the mixture warm.

5 Cook the pasta in plenty of boiling salted water according to the instructions on the packet. Drain well through a colander and toss with a knob of butter.

6 Divide the pasta among four warmed bowls and spoon over the sauce. Sprinkle with grated Parmesan cheese and top with a spoonful of soured cream.

Tagliatelle with Peas, Asparagus and Beans

A creamy pea sauce makes a wonderful combination with crunchy young vegetables.

INGREDIENTS

Serves 4

15ml/1 tbsp olive oil
1 garlic clove, crushed
6 spring onions, sliced
225g/8oz/2 cups frozen peas, thawed
350g/12oz fresh young asparagus
30ml/2 tbsp chopped fresh sage, plus extra leaves to garnish
finely grated rind of 2 lemons
450ml/¾ pint/1¾ cups vegetable stock or water
225g/8oz/2 cups frozen broad beans, thawed
450g/1lb tagliatelle
60ml/4 tbsp low-fat natural yogurt

1 Heat the oil in a pan. Add the garlic and spring onions and cook gently for 2–3 minutes.

2 Add the peas and 115g/4oz of the asparagus, together with the sage, lemon rind and stock or water. Bring to the boil, reduce the heat and simmer for 10 minutes until tender. Purée in a blender or food processor until smooth.

3 Meanwhile remove the outer skins from the thawed broad beans and discard.

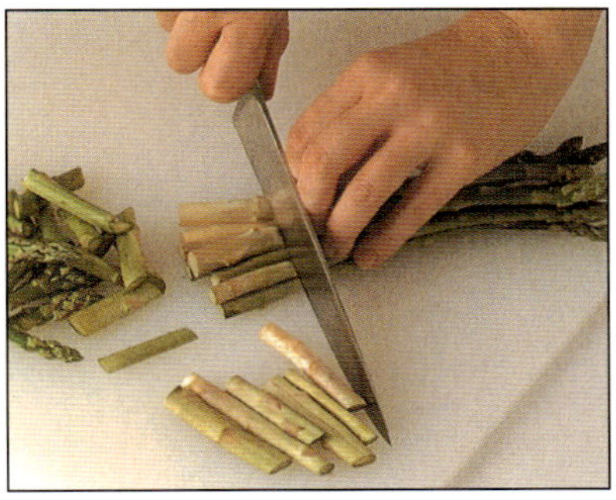

4 Cut the remaining asparagus into 5cm/2in lengths, trimming off any fibrous stems, and blanch in boiling water for 2 minutes.

5 Cook the tagliatelle in plenty of boiling salted water according to the instructions on the packet until *al dente*. Drain well.

6 Add the cooked asparagus and shelled beans to the sauce and reheat. Stir in the yogurt and toss into the tagliatelle. Garnish with sage leaves and serve at once.

Linguine with Sweet Pepper and Cream

The sweetness of red onion complements the peppers in this dish.

INGREDIENTS

Serves 4

1 orange pepper, cored, seeded and cubed
1 yellow pepper, cored, seeded and cubed
1 red pepper, cored, seeded and cubed
350g/12oz linguine
30ml/2 tbsp olive oil
1 red onion, sliced
1 garlic clove, chopped
30ml/2 tbsp chopped fresh rosemary
150ml/¼ pint/⅔ cup double cream
salt and ground black pepper
fresh rosemary sprigs, to garnish

1 Preheat the grill to hot. Place the peppers, skin-side up, on a grill rack. Grill for 5–10 minutes until the skins begin to blister and char, turning occasionally.

2 Remove the peppers from the heat, cover with a clean dish towel and leave to stand for about 5 minutes.

3 Carefully peel away the skins from the peppers and discard. Slice the peppers into thin strips.

4 Cook the pasta in plenty of boiling salted water according to the instructions on the packet.

5 Heat the oil in a frying pan and fry the onion and garlic for about 5 minutes until softened.

6 Stir in the sliced peppers and chopped rosemary and fry gently for about 5 minutes until heated through.

7 Stir in the cream and heat through gently. Season to taste with salt and pepper.

8 Drain the pasta thoroughly and toss in the sauce. Serve immediately, garnished with sprigs of fresh rosemary.

Fusilli with Mascarpone and Spinach

This creamy, green sauce tossed in lightly cooked pasta is best served with plenty of sun-dried tomato ciabatta bread.

INGREDIENTS

Serves 4

350g/12oz pasta spirals, such as fusilli
50g/2oz/¼ cup butter
1 onion, chopped
1 garlic clove, chopped
30ml/2 tbsp fresh thyme leaves
225g/8oz frozen spinach leaves, thawed
225g/8oz/1 cup mascarpone cheese
salt and ground black pepper
fresh thyme sprigs, to garnish

1 Cook the pasta in plenty of boiling salted water according to the instructions on the packet.

2 Melt the butter in a large saucepan and fry the onion for 10 minutes until softened.

3 Stir in the garlic, fresh thyme, spinach and seasoning and heat gently for about 5 minutes, stirring occasionally, until heated through.

4 Stir in the mascarpone cheese and cook gently until heated through. Do not boil.

5 Drain the pasta thoroughly and stir into the sauce. Toss until well coated. Serve immediately, garnished with fresh thyme.

COOK'S TIP

Mascarpone is a rich Italian cream cheese. If you cannot find any, use ordinary full-fat cream cheese instead.

Curly Lasagne with Classic Tomato Sauce

A classic sauce that is simply delicious just served by itself.

INGREDIENTS

Serves 4

30ml/2 tbsp olive oil
1 onion, chopped
30ml/2 tbsp tomato purée
5ml/1 tsp paprika
2 × 400g/14oz cans chopped tomatoes, drained
pinch of dried oregano
300ml/½ pint/1¼ cups dry red wine
large pinch of caster sugar
350g/12oz curly lasagne
salt and ground black pepper
Parmesan cheese shavings, to serve
chopped fresh flat leaf parsley, to garnish

1 Heat the oil in a large frying pan and fry the onion for 10 minutes, stirring occasionally, until softened. Add the tomato purée and paprika and cook for a further 3 minutes.

2 Add the tomatoes, oregano, wine and sugar and season to taste, then bring to the boil.

3 Simmer for 20 minutes until the sauce has reduced and thickened, stirring occasionally.

4 Meanwhile, cook the pasta in plenty of boiling salted water according to the instructions on the packet. Drain thoroughly and turn into a large serving dish. Pour over the sauce and toss to coat. Serve sprinkled with Parmesan cheese shavings and the chopped fresh flat leaf parsley.

COOK'S TIP

If you cannot find curly lasasgne use plain lasagne snipped in half lengthways.

Pasta with Roasted Pepper and Tomato

Add other vegetables such as French beans or courgettes or even chick-peas to make this sauce more substantial, if you like.

INGREDIENTS

Serves 4

2 red peppers
2 yellow peppers
45ml/3 tbsp olive oil
1 onion, sliced
2 garlic cloves, crushed
2.5ml/½ tsp mild chilli powder
400g/14oz can chopped tomatoes
450g/1lb dried pasta shells or spirals
salt and ground black pepper
freshly grated Parmesan cheese, to serve

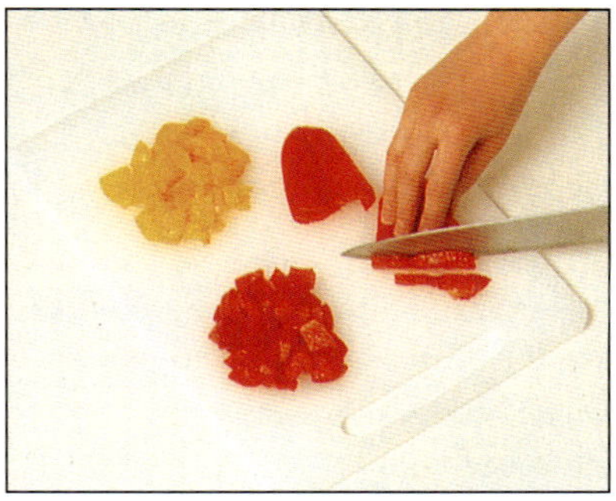

1 Preheat the oven to 200°C/400°/Gas 6. Place the peppers on a baking sheet or in a roasting tin and bake for about 20 minutes or until they are beginning to char. Alternatively you could grill the peppers, turning frequently until evenly blistered.

2 Rub the skins off the peppers under cold water. Halve, seed and roughly chop the flesh.

3 Heat the oil in a medium saucepan and add the onion and garlic. Cook gently for 5 minutes until soft and golden.

4 Stir in the chilli powder, cook for 2 minutes, then add the tomatoes and peppers. Bring to the boil and simmer for 10–15 minutes until the sauce is slightly thickened and reduced. Season.

5 Cook the pasta in plenty of boiling salted water according to the instructions on the packet. Drain well and toss with the sauce. Serve piping hot with plenty of grated Parmesan cheese.

Index